Healing Conflicts in Marriage
MAKING PEACE WITH YOUR PARTNER

OTHER BOOKS BY H. NORMAN WRIGHT

Crisis Counseling
Communication: Key to Your Marriage
Making Peace with Your Past
How to Have a Creative Crisis
Understanding the Man in Your Life
Self-Talk, Imagery, and Prayer (Vol. 3 in the Resources for Christian Counseling Series)

Healing Conflicts in Marriage

MAKING PEACE WITH YOUR PARTNER

H. Norman Wright

WORD BOOKS
PUBLISHER
WACO, TEXAS
A DIVISION OF
WORD, INCORPORATED

MAKING PEACE WITH YOUR PARTNER

Library of Congress Cataloging-in-Publication Data

Wright, H. Norman.
Making peace with your partner.

Bibliography: p.
1. Marriage—United States. 2. Marriage—Religious aspects—Christianity. 3. Interpersonal relations.
I. Title.
HQ734.W9493 1988 646.7'8 88–5553
ISBN 0–8499–3106–1 (pbk.)

Printed in the United States of America
89801239 BKC 987654321

What is the source of quarrels
and conflicts among you?
James 4:1 NASB

Contents

Healing Conflicts in Marriage
MAKING
PEACE
WITH YOUR
PARTNER

"For I know the plans I have for you," says the Lord, "plans for good and not for evil, to give you a future and a hope" (Jeremiah 29:11 AMP).

1

There Is Relief in Sight

That was the weather report that day. 108 degrees! It shouldn't have been that hot on October 4 in Southern California, but it was. The air hung heavy with an oppressive heat that made it hard to breathe. Small wispy vapors of heat rose from the blistering pavement. There wasn't even the slightest breeze. The weather report indicated that it would continue. *No relief in sight!*

It had been a dry year. The annual rainfall level in California had been lower than normal and some areas of the state had to place restrictions on water usage. The level of water in underground caverns and wells was slowly disappearing and serious trouble was believed to be around the corner. Especially if this year's rainfall continued as in previous years. One morning I looked at the three-month forecast to see if we could expect to have the drought broken. The report was not encouraging. It simply said to expect drier than normal conditions. The forecaster's word for it? *No relief in sight!*

Many of my relatives live on farms in South Dakota and Minnesota. Some years bring an excessive amount of snowfall to their part of the country. One of my relatives shared with me his experience: "This one year was almost more than we could take. It never seemed to stop. We would have one major snowfall and then instead of it clearing up enough for us to get out and get the farm functioning again, we would be hit with another storm. And the snow would pile higher and higher. We would make a dent in the clean-up and then several feet more of that cold, wet, white stuff would come down. Even when spring came and we were ready to start plowing, we had a massive blizzard that delayed us for weeks. We were looking forward to the spring weather for a break and that last storm just stopped us cold. It was like—there was *no relief in sight!*"

No relief in sight! I've heard that term before. Not always in regard to the weather, however, but rather, I've heard it in my counseling office. I've heard it from the young, the middle-aged, the elderly, from both men and women. What are these people talking about? In their own way they are giving me a weather report concerning their marriage!

In our Marriage Renewal seminars, at one point we ask every person to draw a weather report depicting their marriage at the present time. They can use all the weather elements to depict what they are currently experiencing in their marriage: bright sunshine, light, wispy or heavy, ominous clouds, a light breeze or the raging winds of a hurricane, a tornado, light snow, hail, and so on. You ought to see some of the completed pictures! They tell a dramatic story.

But what about you? What would a weather report of your marriage say? Naturally it will change from week to week, but are the storm clouds a constant companion or do you experience relief? Some of the marital storms blow over quickly, leaving behind refreshing, brisk breezes and newly gained insights. However, there are other storms that bring devastation and marital destruction. These are like hurricanes. I'm sure you've seen films of these vicious storms or even experienced them. A hurricane carries with it gale-force winds and when it hits the shoreline, it sends towering walls of water inland to create havoc. It doesn't ease in gradually. Rather, it levels whatever lies in its path with overpowering force. Life is turned upside down and into turmoil.

The hurricane passes after a few days, the wind subsides and the warm sun comes out. The rain has stopped but the angry waves continue to pound the beach and even wash inland for awhile. Some of the stormy times of marriage are like that. The marital hurricane is over but deep hurts have been inflicted and there are powerful feelings that continue to surge painfully—long after the storm is gone.

I hear about these weather variations in my office. When the marital upset has been an overwhelming crisis, I hear, "When will this be over? When will the pain and hurt subside?

There's no relief!" Others say, "We just never resolve our problems. We talk about them and bring them up from time to time, but nothing gets resolved. We both know we'll fight about this next week as we've been doing for the last three years! Why do these conflicts have to go on so long?"

That's a good question. Why *do* they? Why *isn't* there any resolution? What happened to the marital life or harmony, fulfillment and satisfaction that you dreamed about when you married? Where is the relief from the disruption and conflict?

I have a message for you. It was given to me to pass on to you in a very simple form. The message is this: THERE IS RELIEF IN SIGHT! Thank God for that. There is relief from past hurts, present pain, conflict, disagreements and disharmony, but you have to *believe* that relief is available. You have to believe that you can change, your partner can change and your marriage can change! Your life can be different and God wants it to be different.

There are two passages in the book of Jeremiah which help me to keep the right perspective, whether the sun is shining brightly or I'm fighting against the force of a hurricane.

> "For I know the plans that I have for you," says the LORD, "plans for good and not for evil, to give you a future and a hope" (Jeremiah 29:11).
>
> "Call to Me, and I will answer you, and I will tell you great and mighty things, which you do not know" (Jeremiah 33:3).

Do you believe that your marriage can be different? Do you believe that it is possible to change? If not, you may be moving toward a life of despair. When hope is absent, despair is on the horizon. And despair looks for solutions other than revitalizing the existing marriage. Your marriage will change for the better or the worse. Do you want to be in charge of that change or have it happen because of default or erosion?

A marriage will change! It is not made up of two immobile, frozen statues who exist side by side. It's made up of two sinners with weaknesses and strengths. Because of the grace and power of God in their lives and the presence of Jesus Christ, they have the greatest chance of anyone to develop a fulfilling, harmonious marriage. But if that is true, why hasn't it already occurred? That's a good question! That's what this book is all about.

Let's say you turned on your TV at the news hour and suddenly I came on the screen as the weather person. Of course you'd be surprised to see me there in the first place but probably even more surprised when you heard what I had to say: "Tonight in place of the normal weather report and forecast, I would like to make a forecast for some of my viewers' marriages. For some of you, the forecast is cloudy skies with a 90 percent chance of thunder and lightning storms developing into tornadoes and hurricanes. There is no telling when they will end. In fact, there will be little relief in sight.

"For other viewers, your marriages will have the normal adjustments and will go through the customary phases, but the weather outlook is brighter and clearer. When storm fronts do appear on the horizon, they will not last long and you will be prepared for them. You will (excuse the pun) weather them well.

"And to add to the weather picture, I can tell you, the viewer, which of you will fit into the stormy forecast and which will fit into the good weather forecast. But that's all the time we have right now. Tune in to the next newscast for more details."

Now, if I signed off like that, the TV set in your room would probably get a boot thrown through it. The TV station would get an irate phone call and I would probably receive an invitation to be the next weather person at the North Pole. So to avoid all the above, let me tell you which couples have the best chance of fitting into the good weather forecast. These are not just my own ideas; they have been gleaned from considerable research over the past few years. But I will have a definite opinion when it comes to the last factor which is my own belief.

I'm not just talking about marriages that stay together. Many of those are simply empty shells. I'm talking about those that last and are fulfilling to both partners. I realize that everyone is looking for the surefire formula for successful marriages. I can't give you a guarantee but I can describe the characteristics of a successful marriage. The term I will use here is "healthy marriage."

1. Healthy marriages reflect the ability of both partners to both change and tolerate such adjustments. Each person is flexible. Too many changes bring disruption with a feeling of being out of control, however. This opens the door for anxieties. But like the captain of a sailing vessel thrown off course by a sudden wave, strong marriages contain people who are able to adjust, make course corrections, and move back to a solid compass setting and remain on their original course. But this also means making personal changes for the benefit of themselves, their partner and their marriage. The big question is: How flexible are you? How flexible is your partner? If I were to ask you to give me some examples to convince me of your flexibility, what would you say?

2. A second characteristic is the ability to live with the unalterable. This includes living without all the answers to life, without having some problems totally resolved. This isn't always easy, especially for men, since they have this burning desire to feel that they are in control of their lives. There will be some personality characteristics and habits which will never be changed. Perhaps your spouse will never remember to put the car seat back to the position you need when you drive. Perhaps you will always put your clothes out the night before which makes the room look cluttered. Perhaps your spouse will always gargle with the door open and miss the sink bowl most of the time. Are these major annoyances? Only if we let them become such. To have a good marriage we must be able to live with the imperfect. We have as our model, God—who loves us in spite of our imperfection.

3. A third and extremely important characteristic is the belief in the permanence of marriage. When couples marry, they enter the relationship with the dream and hope that it will last forever. In premarital counseling sessions I encourage couples always to hold to the belief that their marriage will never end in divorce. Divorce is simply not one of the options. "Till death do us part" is not a heavy, binding chain to bear but a gratifying commitment. This means that during the times of conflict, distance and anger, divorce is not even considered. As one person jokingly put it, "Divorce, no. Murder, maybe." When you hold to the belief that your marriage will last, it affects your approach to an imperfect spouse, your differences

and conflicts, and your future together. Yes, it's true that the commitment level may not be the same for each partner. It may ebb and flow from time to time, but the commitment is there just the same.

4. Trust is another important characteristic for a healthy marriage. As one wife said, "I can depend upon Todd to keep his word. There's no flaking off or setting me up for failure. If he says he will be home at a certain time, he is either there or he calls me. I like that. It gives me a sense of security and I feel freer with him because of that. Our intimacy level is strong because we trust one another." When couples can depend and rely upon one another, they have a rare commodity desperately sought after in today's world.

5. It's interesting that a balance of power is another characteristic. One of the main causes and perpetuators of conflict is the power struggle so common in marriages today. Marriage is based upon the recognition of the strengths and giftedness of each partner—and the freedom to express such in the marriage. It is a marriage of "more or less equal power." Dependency and dominance (both used positively here) shift back and forth.

6. Here's an important characteristic: Each person enjoys his or her partner. This means they enjoy the other's presence, silence, talking, values, faith and so on. In a *Psychology Today* survey done in 1985, the respondents' first choice as to why their marriage was satisfying was, "My spouse is my best friend." Any friendship takes time to cultivate and develop. Such a friendship also implies a loyalty to one another.

7. The couple shares a history together which provides them with a depth of memories and experience to draw on for the future. Not all memories are painless—but they are part and parcel of life and marriage. One memory that Joyce and I share is our over twenty years together with our profoundly retarded son Matthew. We have experienced heartache, pain, grief, joy, delight and growth because of Matthew. These are memories we would not give up for anything. The ability to put whatever happens in our lives into God's perspective will provide the stability that we seek. In a healthy marriage couples share, value and enjoy their history together. They learn to grow from what has occurred rather than to regret.[1]

One other characteristic of a successful marriage is my own bias and in a sense it ties into the previous one. Couples who have the greatest chance of weathering the storms of life are those who have developed a biblical perspective on life. How is this done? You and I were called to belong to God. He wants us for Himself. He also wants us to have a life of joy. Too many of us want to be happy but happiness is usually based upon circumstances. "Happy" comes from the same root word as "happening." But joy! That's something else. Joy defies circumstances and occurs "in spite of . . . ." When we look at the book of Philippians, we find that for Paul, joy is more than a mood or an emotion. Joy is an understanding of life that encompasses both elation and depression. Joy can accept with creative submission events which bring either delight or dismay. Joy allows a person to see beyond any particular event to Jesus Christ who stands above all events.[2]

The most penetrating concept concerning joy was written by James: "Consider it all joy, my brethren, when you encounter various trials, knowing that the testing [or trying] of your faith produces endurance" (James 1:2–3). It's easy to read a passage like this and say, "Well, that's fine." But do you know what the word "consider" actually means? It refers to an internal attitude of the heart or the mind that allows the trial and circumstance of life to affect us adversely or beneficially. Another way James 1:2 might be translated is: "Make up your mind to regard adversity as something to welcome or be glad about."

You have the power to decide what your attitude will be toward any event in your life—including marriage. You can approach it and say, "That's terrible. Totally upsetting. That is the last thing I wanted for my life. Why did it have to happen now? Why me?"

The other way of "considering" the same difficulty is to say: "It's not what I wanted or expected, but it's here. There are going to be some difficult times, but how can I make the best of them?" I'm not going to deny the pain or the hurt that you might have to go through, but eventually we must ask, "What can I learn from it? How can I grow through this? How can I learn from it? How can it be used for God's glory?" These are some of the most important questions of life.

The verb tense used in the word *consider* indicates a decisiveness of action. It's not an attitude of resignation—"Well, I'll just give up. I'm just stuck with this problem. That's the way life is." If you resign yourself, you will sit back and not put forth any effort. The verb tense actually indicates that you will have to go against your natural inclination to see the problem as a negative force. There will be some moments when you won't see it that way at all, and then you'll have to remind yourself: "No, I think there is a better way to respond to this. Lord, I really want You to help me see it from a different perspective. Help me respond to my spouse differently and break out of this power struggle." And then your mind will shift to a more constructive response. This often takes a lot of effort on your part. But it works.

God created us with both the capacity and the freedom to determine how we will respond to those unexpected upsets in marriage. You may honestly wish that a certain problem never occurred between you and your spouse. But you cannot change the fact.

Joy is not necessarily a "good feeling." Rather, it is an attitude of gladness. Joy is a choice and is based upon a choice of attitude. Tim Hansel, a man who has endured intense pain over the past decade, has earned the right to write about joy. His book, *You've Gotta Keep Dancin',* has stimulated my own thinking. His thinking has led me to this conclusion: *Pain and upset in life are inevitable but joy is an option.* Yes, you read that right—*joy is an option.* We can actually miss out on joy by not choosing it. Joy is our choice and it often comes through faithfulness, endurance and some suffering. Lewis Smedes put it so well when he wrote, "You and I were created for joy, and if we miss it, we miss the reason for our existence . . . ."[3]

Is there joy today in your marriage? If not, why? What relationship does your attitude have to the conflicts and differences in your marriage?

Your marriage carries with it the uncanny power for personal growth in a way you never dreamed of experiencing. I'm sure you would like that growth to be painless—like the extraction of a tooth under massive doses of Novocain®. But no one yet has developed a marital Novocain®. It doesn't exist. So get set because some of your change and growth will be painful.

Many couples struggle because their marriage involves more work and effort than they could ever imagine. As one man said, "It's much more effort than I ever bargained for. I wanted a peaceful marriage. Harmony? I'm wondering if all the work and effort are worth the few times of peace and harmony we've ever experienced."

Let me ask you a question. How do you describe the conflicts in your life, in your marriage? Do you ever run out of words to describe what goes on? Do you have a vocabulary that would do justice to what you experience? Underline any of the following synonyms for conflict which you feel describe what it's been like in your own marriage. I discovered these in *The Synonym Finder. Conflict*—The verbs include clash, disagree, discord, be at odds, spar, oppose, contend, lock horns, squabble, feud, bicker, wronged, struggle, tussle. Nouns include struggle, strife, warfare, armageddon, fight, dispute, row, spat, quarrel.

Many couples are surprised by marriage. They are surprised because they enter that relationship woefully unprepared. They are surprised because as they moved toward marriage, their sense of reality was distorted by wishful thinking and fantasy. Some are surprised because they married in spite of unresolved past issues, hoping their partner would be their savior.

Who did you marry? Did you marry the one you thought you married? I heard the story of a man who, after an intense and disappointing disagreement with his wife, was quite frustrated and angry with her. After some time he came in and declared, "Janice, you're not the woman I married!" She turned and looked at him and with a faint smile replied, "I never *was* the woman you thought you married." Are we ever the people our spouses thought we were when we first married? Is our spouse ever the person we thought he or she was when we married? We do tend to marry an illusion, a fantasy, an idealization projected onto a frail human such as ourselves. Perhaps we marry a phantom or a dream, but when we reach out to touch that phantom, there is no substance.

One of the initial adjustments that must occur in marriage is facing the realities of marriage. Conflicts subside when this happens. Facing reality isn't all that bad either.

> People can let go of fantasy if they realize that "reality" is not a code word for "trouble." Among other things, reality means accepting the fun of planning a future with another person you respect and love. It is the joy of living with your best friend and the security of catching a whopping cold and having a spouse on hand to make chicken soup without complaining. Reality is having a disagreement and coming to grips with the notion that you and your spouse may never see eye-to-eye on a number of issues.[4]

If there is ever a place in which we need the grace of God to face life's realities, it's marriage. None of us really has the capability of making it by ourselves. Consider this:

Your marriage will make it not because of what you and your spouse do—it will make it because of the grace of God! You may have married because of your love for the other person, but none of us knew what that love was all about. Perhaps we hoped our courtship love would sustain and carry us throughout the years of marriage. We were hoping to relax and enjoy our love. Mike Mason has written one of the most thought-provoking books I have read in the last decade. He says,

> To be married is not to be taken off the front lines of love, but rather, to be plunged into the thick of things. It is to be faced, day in and day out, with the necessity of making over and over again, and at deeper and deeper levels, that same terrifyingly momentous and impossible decision which one could only have made when one was head over heels in love and out of one's mind with trust and faith. This is not resignation to a fate, but the free and spontaneous embracing of a gift, of a challenge and a destiny.
>
> Is it any wonder if people cannot take the pressure? It is a pressure that can only be handled by love, and in ever-increasing doses. Marriage involves a continuous daily renewal of a decision which, since it is of such a staggering order as to be humanly impossible to make, can only be made through the grace of God.[5]

At first couples blissfully assume their partner wants nothing more than to act and think and feel exactly as they do. And when they discover this is not the case, it seems as though something terrible has occurred. But not really. This mourning carries with it the acceptance of differences in character, personality, communication style, values and sexual desire. Eventually acceptance and adjustment lessen conflict. I would rather see some conflict occur so resolution happens instead of burying issues until they rise again out of control, infused with new power and eventually pain.

The storms in your marriage have various starting points. They may be there because of your past experience with your parents. They may be present because you entered marriage believing in too many myths. They may be there because of not knowing how to grow and develop new ways of responding at the present time. No matter what the reasons, you can overcome those hindrances.

What were your myths about marriage? I have heard many from couples who have been in my office. Some of the more common myths are:

"I thought my spouse would be an extension of my own emotional and physical needs. And when my needs weren't met right away and in the way I wanted, I felt ripped off! I got angry! How dare that person not meet my needs!"

"I expected my marriage to be problem free. After all, good Christian marriages just don't have problems or conflict. Nobody told me that good marriages become good marriages through constructive conflict."

"I expected my spouse to know what I wanted or needed. Why spend a lot of time talking about what you want? Once you're married, they ought to know."

And the list goes on. What myths or misbeliefs did you carry into marriage? What happened to them? Did they die? Did they receive a proper burial or do they go through a periodic resurrection?

Some people never get out of the mourning stage of marriage. Perhaps that statement strikes you as strange but part of the transitional growth pattern of marriage is mourning the death of the unrealistic marital dreams.

As Mel Krantzler puts it:

> So many people experience marriage as entrapment, as a never-ending series of onerous obligations which cause a

husband and wife to feel they count for little in each other's eyes. They see themselves as passive and helpless and, therefore, unable to change the roles, or the relationship. A woman tells me, "I feel I've been to obedience school in the ten years of my marriage, and I've yet to receive my diploma!" And a man complains about his fifteen-year marriage, "It seems like I've always been the executor of my wife's will!"

> It is not the institution of marriage, but the way in which people view their marriage and react toward each other that generates this condition. There is no need to despair or wallow in this state of affairs, since this condition is self-created. And since it is self-created, it can be changed for the better, no matter how long you have been married. Every couple has the personal power to recreate their marriage and transform it into the kind of loving relationship that they want with each other. Marriage is the one area in modern life in which every couple has the total power to shape its course for better or for worse. As such, it should be considered a gift instead of a gift horse, for it offers each of us the opportunity to stretch our abilities, to use them more effectively than we have done previously.[6]

You're probably looking for some new and profound solutions this time. What I have to offer is not new nor is it my own. All through this book suggestions and guidelines will be shared. But I do want to give you a formula at this time which can cut through the most major or minor problems, the most recent and most lingering of conflicts that you may be experiencing. I didn't write it, Paul did. And it wasn't his own inspiration either. God said it. Here's the formula for anyone who is married: "Let all bitterness and wrath and anger and clamor and slander be put away from you, along with all malice. And be kind to one another, tender-hearted, forgiving each other, just as God in Christ also has forgiven you" (Ephesians 4:31–32).

This is the formula to help you handle the upset and tension in your marriage. This is the formula for preventing conflicts in your relationships. I have seen hundreds of couples, who, if they had learned to live their lives according to this passage would never have had to make an appointment with me.

Bitterness comes into our lives as we harbor the hurts, disappointments, rejections and unresolved conflicts that we've experienced with our partner. We push the pain of these experiences deep within us and soon the feeling of ill will and desire for revenge begins to flavor our attitude and actions. And if we give vent to our bitterness by speaking bitterly, we only create a deep feeling of alienation.

Wrath is the uncontrolled temper which causes us to act without thinking of the consequences. Have you seen the marks and bruises on a person's face which came as a result of the wrath of her partner? I have. It's not a pretty sight and it's a violation of God's creation. Wrath has been described as wind in violent motion like a tornado or hurricane. I once saw winds of seventy miles per hour destroy the fence on our property. I have seen the results of a freak tornado in Long Beach uproot several substantial trees on our street. It's scary. Wrath is scary for it is an inner conflict that is out of control.

Anger is a strong response or irritation or upset. It pushes one's partner away rather than drawing them close. It often creates the very response we are desperately trying to eliminate.

Clamor is a response with little restraint and it has no regard for the feelings or condition of one's spouse. I often see examples of the "slander" spoken of in this passage. I see it happening before my eyes as one spouse casts aspersions on the partner's values, beliefs and character. Sometimes I sit in amazement and wonder how people can take some of the verbal abuse they do.

Malice is an interesting term. It reflects a person's mindset and in this case it is a mind bent upon doing less than the best for the other person. Malice is spite, ill will or baseness of any kind.

You and I have been called to put away these responses. If they occur we cannot blame our spouse since we are responsible for our own responses regardless of how our partner acts. You and I have been called to reflect the presence of Jesus Christ in our lives. This occurs when we are kind, tenderhearted and forgiving toward our partner.

When this Ephesians passage becomes so much a part of you that you don't even have to think about putting it into practice, you have a tool which will affect your relationships dramatically. There will be other passages and suggestions to add to this beginning you are making. Your marriage does not have to be a downhill glide of disenchantment. Marital growth and fulfillment can be maintained for ten, twenty, thirty, forty and fifty years or more. You and your partner can create the quality in your marriage that you seek. You cannot do it by yourself. You cannot do it together. But you can do it by the grace of God, and by inviting Jesus Christ to be the head of your relationship, you can do it by deriving your security and identity from Him. There is good news. THERE IS RELIEF IN SIGHT!

Life-Changers

—*Joy is an option.*

—*God's grace will enable you to make that daily commitment.*

—*Experience the excitement of living out Ephesians 4:31–32.*

Instead in the true spirit of humility, (lowliness of mind) let each regard the others as better than and superior to himself—thinking more highly of one another than you do of yourselves. Let each of you esteem and look upon and be concerned for not merely his own interests, but also each for the interests of others (Philippians 2:3, 4 AMP).

2

Who's Running Your Life?

The alarm goes off with a shrill ring. Your hand reaches out and without thinking you hit the button. With half-opened eyes, you climb out of bed and head toward the bathroom. On the way, you slip your feet into slippers, grab a robe with your left hand and swing your right hand and arm into the sleeve. On your way out of the bedroom, you give your spouse a poke to make him get up and then you shut the bathroom door. With your left hand you grab the toothbrush and with your right, the toothpaste—all in one easy motion.

After the bathroom, you walk into the kitchen and nod to the dog. Your left hand automatically flips on the coffee maker which was stocked from the night before. Your right hand opens the refrigerator and grabs the orange juice. With your left foot, you nudge open the door of the cupboard and flip out a dog biscuit for the pooch. He says "thank you" with a wag of his tail and you move on to the next task of putting some toast in the toaster. The next 20 minutes is a carbon copy of the over 168 small but important behaviors which get you ready to face the hard, cruel world.

Did you think about each behavior? Did you have to talk yourself into doing this and then doing that? Of course not! These actions just came naturally to you. You had been programmed. As you did each little act for so many years they became automatic. In fact, each morning when you arise, you shift into automatic and begin to function. Do you know what we call these actions? Habits! You have trained yourself well.

We need to develop some habits, especially those that help us get through the day. Some habits are beneficial and some are crippling. We tend to have both.

You're a creature of habit . . . and so am I. You may not like to hear that and prefer thinking you're flexible. But most of what we think, say or do comes from habits we've developed. They're always in operation whether we're aware of them or not. What we've learned, we tend to practice and this is what we become.

If one drives the same way to work each day for twenty years, he does not have to think about routes. In fact, one day I took off on the freeway to go to the Orange County Airport. The first part of the freeway was the route to work and instead of turning on to a different freeway, ten miles later I realized that I was on the way to my office instead of being on the right road to the airport. That's habit! Sometimes I wonder who's in the driver's seat of my life. Who's in the driver's seat of your life? You or some habit?

Remember this about habits: As much as 98 percent of what we do is the result of habit rather than choice. Habits operate outside the conscious mind whereas choice is in the conscious mind.

Whatever you do again and again becomes a habit. If you react with anger to your spouse's concerns or requests, it will become a habit. If you turn off your spouse when you don't care for what is being said, it will become a habit. What you practice, you become.

What you practice, you also become good at. Some spouses become good at arguing, defending, criticizing, being caustic, blocking feelings, pulling the silent treatment, being a workaholic, being abusive. Are you aware of what it takes to change a habit? Even to make a small positive behavior a part of your repertoire of behaviors will take *at least* a minimum of eighteen repetitions over a period of eighteen days for it to have a chance to lock into your system.

But negative habits are not what the Scriptures encourage us to become good at doing! I've had people share with me that they are professional worriers. They have been worrying for so long they are good at it. And I tend to believe them. Even worry takes practice and then it becomes automatic.

Every living thing will fight to the death to stay alive. So? Habits are living things, so expect resistance. You gave your habit life by practicing—and it wants to stay in control. You've invaded its country and it's going to try to repel you. Change is a massive battle and it must be fought on your terms, namely the celebration of *new* behaviors rather than *old* negative habits.[1]

Do you feel that your habits are your master? Paul talked about who is your master in Romans 6:12–23. He also described the battle of doing what we don't want to do and not doing what we want to do. It's like a war and when you confront a habit you have declared war within yourself. You will feel tension and at times even take out the white flag of surrender as you feel overrun and overwhelmed by those deeply entrenched habits. But rejoice! You can change. *You can change your habit patterns or response to your spouse and it has nothing to do with how he or she behaves.*

Why are power struggles and negative reinforcement patterns difficult to change? There are two main reasons that can be applied to other areas of our lives as well. *We reinforce our negative self-defeating behavior by believing and making the statement, "It's hard to change." We tend to be locked into our habits and they do take time and energy to change.*

Our habits have three main functions. Do you know the difference between a thermometer and a thermostat? A thermometer *records* the environment but a thermostat *controls* it. Habits tend to be our personal "reality thermostats." They keep the environment comfortable by compelling us to act the way we see ourselves. Since we are comfortable with routine, our thermostats tend to go to work if we begin to stray from our habit patterns.

Try driving to work by a different route than the one you've followed for years. Is it comfortable or is there a tendency to revert back to your old pattern? If you're normal, you'll tend to revert—even if your routine is uncomfortable. That's why so many couples continue to bicker and argue and quarrel in the same manner. Isn't that strange? Your thermostat is your source of power. It gives you feelings of being in control.

A second function of a habit tendency is that it activates a feeling which we use to determine how to respond and act. We have learned which behaviors feel normal and which do not. And there is the problem—our habits are ties into our feelings. Feelings only face backwards—they know what *was*—but not what could be! Feelings cannot be our guide for breaking out of marital patterns that are unfulfilling. There will be no new behavior if we allow our feelings to be our guide.

I am not against feelings. They're an important part of our lives and we need to listen to them. They add a new beauty and depth to life. But when connected to habits, they tend to lead us down the wrong path. Our feelings can change, but that comes about by changing how we act and how we think. One must practice the change as long as it takes for the new behavior to become as comfortable as the old behavior.

If there is one principle I would like you to remember from this section on habits, it is this: *You cannot expect different results from the same old behavior—new results come from new behavior!* So, why keep on engaging in the same old patterns! Think about it! There has to be a better way! But remember, since our habits are alive, they are going to fight to stay alive!

The third function of a habit is to help one determine his own interpretation of reality. Habits are like emotional glasses through which we decide what's real and what isn't. If we've had a lot of disappointments in life, we may tend to view all of life as one big disappointment and expect new ones to occur. We may feel that all of life is one big struggle. I may believe that I won't or can't change, nor can my spouse. What happens then? My belief will turn out to be self-fulfilling prophecy. These glasses are distorted for they interpret life and reality in a closed, limited way. But again, they're comfortable, aren't they![2]

Now let's consider a far too common type of marital relationship which can lend itself to dissatisfaction as a result of habits. I'm talking about domination and control.

Power and control issues can emerge between all couples. These are major conflicts for many couples. But some individuals have a greater need to control and some a greater need to be controlled. I'm sure you're aware of the terms *submissive, passive* and *dependent.* Each term is tied into the others. Perhaps by now you've discovered if you or your partner is dependent. All of us have an inclination toward dependency. At times we all wish that someone would take care of us in some way. But when a person is totally dependent, he or she lives in fear of abandonment and tends to be possessive. This person has an excessive need for reassurance that he or she is lovable. And, unfortunately, dependent people tend to respond too quickly to affection and caring. They frequently enter a marriage without considering the qualities of their partner. Some dependent people allow destructive patterns since the need for love and closeness is so strong. Unwittingly, they cooperate with vicious circles and in passive ways contribute to some power struggles.

Dependent people are often called pleasers. Women tend to be more dependent than men and are frequently the pleasers in a relationship.

Every pleaser is unique, but there are common threads in their lives. Some of the major characteristics are these:

1. They learned to be pleasers when they were children. Often pleasers tend to be perfectionists who respond very well to parental pressure.

2. They often come from unhappy homes in which father gave them little attention, love or support. Unfortunately they never learned how to relate to a male in a positive healthy manner. And this deficit is carried with them into their marriage. Fathers have such an influence upon a woman's development. (See my book, *Understanding the Man in Your Life,* chapter 3, "The First Man in Your Life.")

3. Pleasers tend to settle for small favors. They may be frustrated, but put up with it. They may be inwardly angry, but believe it could be worse. They are comfortable with their unhappiness and misery.

4. The major common characteristic is low self-esteem. They rarely feel they are worth much and must earn their value and worth. Thus the overemphasis to please.

5. They try to keep everyone happy and the waters smooth. "Please don't be upset, let's have peace" is their cry.

6. Pleasers usually feel inferior to men and act so that men approve of them. They learn to be obedient to authority figures.[3]

Some women are pleasers because they feel unworthy. They think they lack something and feel an excessive need to have others love them. This is a response coming from a position of weakness. Others are pleasers because this is a logical choice for them. They can be assertive and feel good about themselves. They do not allow others to dominate or run over them. This is a healthy choice and response coming from a position of strength. In his book *The Pleasers—Women Who Can't Say No, and the Men Who Control Them,* Dr. Kevin Leman discusses the pleaser in a carefully detailed manner. He has an interesting description for the various types of pleasers:

Positive Pleaser—Good balance between pleasing nature and receiving the respect, support and love she wants and needs.

Mildly Discouraged Pleaser—Pluses usually outweigh the minuses, but she knows life could be a great deal better if she knew how to get the world to show her a little more respect.

Played-out (Exhausted) Pleaser—Making a go of life, but feeling stressed out, tired and fatigued. She can't say no, and always has to do the giving in any relationship.

Depressed Pleaser—Hurt, miserable and unhappy, often connected to a loser or womanizer, whom she feels she has to care for and help. (Occupationally, the Depressed Pleaser is often a nurse or other professional care-giver.) May need professional help.

Supersuffering Pleaser—In real pain, probably has relationship with a misogynist, needs professional help.[4]

The controllers, who are they! Us! We all have some tendency or desire to control. After all, one of our basic desires is to *feel* as though we are in control at all times. But those who have the need to always be in control actually feel out of control of one very important segment of their lives. Do you know what that might be? It's feelings. This leads them to try to control the way other people feel. They want others to like them and love them. They have a tremendous need to be in charge. Naturally, they make the decisions. Such people overwhelm and intimidate their spouses which in time can destroy their partner's feelings for them. (This is true of men *and* women.) The very thing they want they destroy. The very thing they don't want to happen, they create. They fear abandonment. This is why they attempt to control others in the first place. Both dependent and controlling spouses fear abandonment. Their style of trying to keep it from happening varies.

If you've ever met a controlling person you probably know they have to be right, have to win, have to have the last word and appear blameless. Their way is the right way and if mistakes happen, they look for a scapegoat. Any attempt to criticize them is met with a stronghold of resistance. They also tend to belittle their accomplishments and laugh at their feelings.

How do you prove that you love this person? Simple. Obedience. "Obey me and I know you love me," is their cry. They often feel unappreciated and unencouraged—and why not? Who would want to help the controller become even more of a controller?

Controllers are unhappy and dissatisfied people. They are easily and deeply hurt. But they would not want you to know it. Admitting pain would seem weak and vulnerable, and this might invite rejection. The tragedy of the controller is that he goes through life feeling alone and isolated since he cannot allow himself to be vulnerable. Intimacy in a marriage where a controller resides is nonexistent. Neither the controller nor a dependent person will run the risk of opening up because of fear of the other person. And thus trust is also very low in this type of a marriage.[5]

A controller-dependent marriage has its own balance and maintains a level of comfort. Why? Because the needs of each are being fulfilled even though it's unhealthy. But if the dependent person begins to pull away or mature and become assertive, the balance is upset. Then the controller tends to tighten the clamps. If the controller cannot commit to change, the relationship often breaks up. This is when the power struggles break out into the open. They have been there but beneath the surface. One tries to dominate and control, and the only recourse the dependent person has is to go underground and become a passive manipulator. But when growth occurs the power issues break out into the open!

By the way, controllers do end up marrying other controllers. I have worked with many of them. Power struggles are a constant companion. These relationships take a great deal of mutual respect, understanding and acceptance. If one individual is less gifted than the other—or less mature—control becomes a major issue and the marriage often deteriorates.[6]

I am making a distinction between a person of strength and a controller. Mature individuals have strengths and capabilities and know it. But they also have weak spots and know that, too. They like to lead but can defer to others. They encourage others and are not threatened by others' capabilities. Not so with the controller.

Dr. Kevin Leman believes that possibly the most common marriage relationship today is the pleasing wife and the controlling husband. Some of these work well as long as the two remain in that posture, or if the controller is more a man of strength and the pleaser has made a mature choice regarding that role. But many are not and misery soon prevails. Here is Dr. Leman's match-up of the characteristics of the two spouses:

The Pleaser	*The Controller*
Low self-esteem—always working hard to please and earn acceptance.	Capitalizes by keeping the pleaser off balance—in her place. He knows her soft spots, her Achilles' heel.
Often from a family that did not meet her emotional needs—particularly her father.	Incredibly, the pleaser seems inevitably drawn toward a man like her father—the familiar is somehow more attractive than what could be fulfilling and comfortable.
A fixer and reformer—she knows she can change him.	His "weaknesses" are what make the relationship go. If she could really "fix him," he'd probably be dull and uninteresting.

The Pleaser	*The Controller*
Tendency to fantasize—failure to grasp reality.	He seems to have a firm grasp on reality and everything else—especially the pleaser.
Quick to take the blame—she "knows it's all her fault."	He is quite willing to let her play the blame game—as long as she is always the loser.
Thankful for small favors—life could be worse.	He knows she'll put up with him—in fact, he's counting on it. He knows he's "got her in his pocket."
Has the Avis Complex—always trying harder.	And as she "dances on eggs," he plays the tune.
Doesn't feel worthy of real love or respect.	He knows he can lie and be overbearing and demanding because she'll take it—she "expects it."
God is nonexistent or a distant, dangerous judge or policeman who disapproves of her most of the time.[7]	Since controllers like to play god, she is playing right into his hands.

The controller-dependent relationship is *not* what the Bible calls for! The call to marriage is not a call to control, dictate or dominate. The call to marriage is a calling to servanthood. All believers are called to be servants. On six occasions in the Gospels we see that the greatest must be a servant (Matthew 20:26–28, 23:11; Mark 9:35, 10:43–45; Luke 9:48, 22:26–27). Paul has nine verses exhorting husbands to love their wives. In fact, a man is to love his wife with a sacrificial servant love. Marriage is a partnership of equals in which each contributes his or her strengths to the other's weaknesses in a mutual ministry to one another.

The scripture does talk about authority and submission as a clear choice of those to whom the passages were written. Yes, the scripture does talk about the husband being the head—but this does not mean a tyrannical, authoritarian controller. He is primarily responsible for creating a partnership of equals under one responsible head. Spouses are to regard one another as equal partners in everything that concerns their life together. The headship of the man carries the task of seeing that the equal partnership is kept inviolable. A loving husband affirms, defers, shares, encourages and stimulates. Loving headship delights to delegate without demanding. Charlie Shedd suggests that marriage under the biblical order is like a conductor leading a symphony rather than a potentate ruling over his realm!

In a marriage the person to be controlling each partner is Jesus Christ. He is the head of each person. As Philippians 2:6–7 states, he took the form of a servant. The solution to the problem of power struggles in marriage is found in Philippians 2:3–8:

> Do nothing from factional motives—through contentiousness, strife, selfishness or for unworthy ends—or prompted by conceit and empty arrogance. Instead, in the true spirit of humility (lowliness of mind) let each regard the others as better than and superior to himself—thinking more highly of one another than you do of yourselves. Let each of you esteem and look upon and be concerned for not merely his own interests, but also each for the interests of others. Let this same attitude and purpose and [humble] mind be in you which was in Christ Jesus.—Let Him be your example in humility—Who, although being essentially one with God and in the form of God [possessing the fullness of the attributes which make God God], did not think this equality with God was a thing to be eagerly grasped or retained; But stripped Himself [of all privileges and rightful dignity] so as to assume the guise of a servant in that He became like men and was born a human being. And after He had appeared in human form He abased and humbled Himself [still further] and carried His obedience to the extreme of death, even the death of [the] cross! (AMP).

In place of the controlling or the dependent style, there is another option available for both men and women. This style lessens the pain and hurt and conflicts of a marriage. As we have discussed, it's the servanthood style. It means that both partners value themselves and their spouse as a child of God. It means there is a dependency but it is on Jesus Christ. It means each person is encouraged to be him- or herself and develop the giftedness God has given to him or her through this approach. Conflicts are healed.

Life-Changers

Believe that you can change your habits.
Find your strength through healthy servanthood.

Therefore if any man is in Christ, he is a new creature; the old things passed away; behold, new things have come (2 Corinthians 5:17).

3

"There Has to Be a Better Way!"

"If what you're doing isn't working, why keep on doing it? There has to be a better way!"

I probably make this statement 50–100 times a year to couples I see in counseling. They describe the way they interact in their marriage and then discover each of them has been responding in the same manner for the past several years. And it hasn't been working. Why? Why do we continue with the same ineffective patterns and responses instead of trying new approaches? Why aren't people willing to be risk-takers and try a new approach?

On one hand we say, "I would love to change my life"; "I would love to see some changes occur in my marriage"; "I would give anything to get rid of the conflicts in my marriage and have some peace and harmony"; "I would give anything if he/she would just change!"

But would we really? Are we willing to pay the price of change? Do we really believe that change is possible? What about you? Do you *want* to change? Many individuals don't. And many do, but they fail to take the steps necessary for it to happen. Listen to their reasons:

A major hurdle for lack of improvement is the lack of *skill.* As one man said, "I know what I want, but I don't know how to go about making it happen." Many conflicts occur because people do not know how to improve the relationship.

Another reason is *pride.* In many marriages both parties feel as though they are the victim. Why should a victim take the first step in changing? Most victims see this as giving in to their spouse. The act of changing carries with it the implication that they, not their spouse, are either in the wrong, or that they want to be taken advantage of! And what if their partner responds with either greater demands or, worse yet, greater anger?

Yes, there are other reasons which tend to cripple progress. In the previous chapter, we considered the effect of habits. But, rather than focus on the reasons, it is more important to look at one's own relationship and ask the questions, "What is keeping our relationship from growing? What might *I* be doing to keep it from improving? What do *I* need to do at this time as the first step?" Too often we focus on the responsibility of our partner first, and this usually ends in disaster. A partner is more likely to change when he/she sees the other taking the initiative and setting the pattern. This isn't to say that the other party has no need to change.

Many people carry around a pessimistic view of change: "I've tried, but it just can't be done." Some refuse to change because they fear their own inadequacy. Even if their marriage isn't the best and there's conflict, there is also stability. They know what to expect. Unfortunately, many of us fear the unknown aspect of change. Whenever you make any kind of change, you disrupt stability.

Over the years I have had people talk to me about the difficulty of accepting changes in their partner, even when the change was desired!

A common concern on the part of wives is how to get their tight-lipped, closed-mouth, unexpressive husbands to share feelings. One wife talked about the various traumas or crises her husband went through which plunged him into a deep depression. After his treatment he became a very open, emotionally expressive person. But then his wife began to withdraw and seemed uncomfortable with both his questions and what he was saying about himself. He had become the kind of person she wanted him to be, but it seems she felt safer being upset and making demands for him to change rather than with the actual change itself.

Couples are known to set their own "emotional thermostat." They know how cold or hot or how close or distant they want their marriage to be. If one turns the thermostat up, the other turns it down to get it back into balance. When one person changes, the balance is broken and they both need to adjust. They do this by actually reversing roles. The one who was eager to get close draws away and vice versa. Another option is to reset the thermostat to a different emotional level. But remember, when your partner makes that desired alteration, you too will need to change.[1]

We learn to be comfortable with both what we have and what we are. This even includes the pain of an unfulfilled marriage. At least for a time!

The reason for the statement at the beginning of this chapter is this: *I see many people who are more comfortable and secure in their misery than in the possibility of a better relationship.* How tragic! They can't predict the new relationship, so they feel threatened. But there has to be a better way!

The funny thing is, change is going to occur whether you want it to happen or not. It's part of life. It's inevitable. Why pretend that it isn't going to occur? Wouldn't it be better to have a voice in the change? Wouldn't it be better for you to take control rather than letting it just happen to you?

Making a change does not mean failure. It's simply a statement that the way you have been responding has been effective up to a certain point and has helped you live on a certain level. Now you want to live life in an even *more* effective manner. It's a sign of maturity to admit that you want your life and your marriage to be different. Changing means you believe in the future and you *want* a future! It means you are adapting to new situations and you want to grow rather than stagnate.

Yes, change is risky. Yes, some changes can make matters worse for awhile or even permanently. But the likelihood that *positive* changes will occur is high.

You can bring about changes in your life. You can bring about changes in your marriage. You can learn to respond in such a way that your partner will choose to make changes in his or her life as well! Yes—I believe that we can effect change in another person but not by begging, pleading, crying, punishing, becoming irate or threatening. We consume so much emotional and physical energy in our endeavors to change others. But *we all* (including myself) would benefit from making some changes in our own lives. But how? I like the way marriage therapist Martin Padovani describes the process. He says:

> In an initial counseling session with a couple struggling with a marital problem, I see them locked into a bind. Neither trusts the other. They are defensive. They blame each other. They are afraid. Neither is willing to change what he or she can change. Their unhappy relationship pattern will usually begin to change when one of the spouses has the courage to do so. Always very mysterious and marvelous to see, the relationship changes when one person changes.
>
> The one who changes influences the other in one of two ways: by breaking up the unhealthy pattern of behavior between the two, because one refuses to take part in the games being played, ceases the power struggle, and therefore finds a new way of relating; or one person is moved to change because of the change in the other. Mutual trust is restored; the uncaring spouse becomes sincere and caring. When we change what we can in ourselves, we tend to influence others positively in one way or another. The healing power that one possesses to change for the better in a relationship is often beyond our comprehension.[2]

You may think, *Maybe I can change, but fat chance of my spouse changing!* Perhaps you've tried until you're blue in the face. Perhaps you feel your partner is incorrigible. I have had sincere doubts about some relationships and people I've seen, too. But I was wrong. I believe people have a greater capacity for change than we believe. Others are freer to change when the initial modification occurs in our own lives. This change could be in the way we think, speak, behave or confront. It could include creating positive, well-thought-out crises, or simply doing the unexpected—something that is just not for you. It could involve going for counseling by yourself or with the other person. A number of methods will be suggested in this book which are effective. But there is no guarantee on any approach. Beware of those programs which claim success if you just follow their guidelines and suggestions to the letter! This creates a sense of guilt and failure if the desired outcome is not attained. The greatest potential you have is seeing change occur in your own life which creates the conditions for your partner to change!

Let me give you an example that one of my Marriage Seminar couples shared with me.

Jim and Sandra had been married for several years. Jim was quite a neat, meticulous man in just about every area of his life except . . . you guessed it! When it came to picking up after himself around the home he was, in his own words, "kind of sloppy." He shared with me that he would leave towels on the floor in the bathroom and other personal items never seemed to make it into the clothes hamper. Sandra had mentioned to him on numerous occasions how nice it would be if he could pick them up himself or put them in their proper place before they reached the floor. Jim would respond in a fairly positive way, but somehow the message never brought about a change.

One day Jim came back to his office just before lunch time and to his amazement Sandra was in his office with a surprise lunch for him. He noticed that the lights were off, candles were on his desk and his favorite foods were waiting for him. They ate together and enjoyed the time. Sandra then presented him with a wrapped package and asked him to open it. He did and to his astonishment he found a folded towel and underwear under the wrapping. Sandra put her arm around Jim, smiled and said, "Jim, I notice how neat and organized your office is, including your desk. I know you are a man of excellent organizational ability and deep concern for being precise and orderly. I just *know* that you would gain a sense of even deeper satisfaction each day and each night knowing that before you left the house or retired for the night, you could reflect back and remember that when you finished with a towel you placed it thoughtfully and carefully in the clothes hamper along with any underwear which needs to reside there. I'm sure that would really give you a good feeling about yourself and make your day. Thank you for listening. I'll see you this evening." And with that she smiled, picked up the clothes, took her picnic basket and left the office.

Jim was totally taken off guard and had a grin on his face for several hours. From time to time he would shake his head, smile and look as though he were talking to himself.

As they concluded telling me their story, they both added, "That was six months ago and the towels and underwear haven't hit the floor yet." Jim concluded with, "She sure got my attention, I wasn't aware of the impact until three weeks later when I realized I had changed my pattern."

It's time to stop thinking about what we *can't* change in our lives and our marriage and why it *can't* be done and put forth some effort to make some changes happen! You can be in charge of the change! What would *you* like to change in your marital relationship at this time? What would you like *your spouse* to change in your marital relationship at this time?

When we say change isn't possible, we have given up, lost hope and chosen to live a life with phrases of "Why try?"; "Give up"; "They won't ever be different"; "I won't ever be different." Where does all this change begin? What's the starting point? In Charles Swindoll's challenging book, *Living above the Level of Mediocrity,* he talks about:

> How people choose to live a life of mediocrity and follow the herd. But periodically we bump into a few refreshing souls, who have decided that they aren't going to live in the swamp of the status quo, or run scared of being different, even though others will always say, "It can't be done." Those who aim high are strong-willed eagle types who refuse to be bothered by the negativism and skepticism of the majority. They never even use the words, "Let's just quit!" They are the same ones who believe that mediocrity must be confronted. And that confrontation must first take place in the MIND—the seed plot of endless and limitless possibilities.[3]

The *first element* in the process of change then is your mind. Your mind is the source of your words, your behavior and many of your emotional responses. Remember what happened when you accepted Christ? You became a new creation in Jesus Christ. You are now identified with Him. In 2 Corinthians 5:17 Paul says: "Therefore if any man is in Christ, he is a new creature: the old things passed away; behold, new things have come." Then in Romans 6:6 he said: ". . . Our old self was crucified with Him. . . that we should no longer be slaves . . . ."

By believing in Jesus Christ, we died with Him and have been raised a new creation with Him. All things are new—including our thought life. But how can one's mind—one's thought life, the influence of past experiences—become new in one's experience now? First Corinthians 2:16 tells us, ". . . We have the mind of Christ." In 1 Corinthians 1:30 we read, "But by His doing you are in Christ Jesus, who became to us wisdom from God, and righteousness, and sanctification, and redemption." You and I have the *wisdom* of God. Put this thought together with the fact that we have the mind of Christ: *Not only do I have the mind of Christ, but I also have God's wisdom to apply in using the mind of Christ in my life.* Remember? There has to be a better way . . . and this is it!

"It is true that we live in the world, but we do not fight from worldly motives. The weapons we use in our fight are not the world's weapons but God's powerful weapons, which we use to destroy strongholds. We destroy false arguments; we pull down every proud obstacle that is raised against the knowledge of God; we take every thought captive and make it obey Christ" (2 Corinthians 10:3–5, TEV).

This is very important to your marriage. Why? Because you and I came into life with a mind that has been affected by the fall of man. We begin life with a mind that has a propensity toward negative thinking, worry, fear, guilt and remembering experiences that would be better off relinquished. Even when we become believers, the residue of old thinking is still with us. It tends to bring its influence into play with our wills, our emotions, our thoughts and our behavior. And a marriage relationship is the playground where these tendencies can romp.

The healing of some marital conflicts and destructive patterns is difficult because of the defenses we have built around ourselves to keep us from directly confronting our responsibilities. In our minds we raise a drawbridge to keep the pain out, but we end up keeping our spouse away from us as well. This limits us from enjoying deep intimacy, trust and love. Loneliness in marriage is one of the most painful forms of isolation. Raising the drawbridge does not make our castle more secure; rather it turns our sanctuary into a dungeon. To heal the hurts of our relationship, we must lower the drawbridge by giving up our defensiveness and confronting what isn't working.

Because of the presence of Christ in our lives, we can let down the drawbridge. He gives us two possibilities for growth and happiness: First, He changes the old patterns by eliminating the effects of prior hurts in our marriage. Second, He helps us use our minds, emotions and wills to behave in a new, more positive way, both now and in the future.

Our task then, through Christ, is to remove the rough edges and fissures that drain our energy and keep us from moving forward. And it begins in our minds. The Scriptures are so clear on this. The Bible tells us that as a man thinks so is he (Proverbs 23:7). Paul tells us we need a spiritual mind (Romans 8:6), a renewed mind (Ephesians 4:23), a transformed mind (Romans 12:2), a Christlike mind (1 Corinthians 2:11) and a sound mind (2 Timothy 1:7). If you want both joy in your life and the possibility of change in your marriage, the answer is transformed thinking.

But let me suggest a *second element* involved in change which you may not be expecting. It's called *praise*. Praise for what God has done, for who He is and what He will do, releases to Him the tight control we have had on our lives and marriage.

I know it is easy to praise God for what He has done, because we can reflect back and measure the actual results. We have something tangible, and there is little risk involved.

But what do you expect of the future for you and your marriage? Is it difficult for you to praise God for what He is going to do? Praise opens your life to some possibilities you may have never considered. By praising God, you not only become a risk-taker, a change-maker, but you become more aware of what He wants for you. This may be an uncomfortable idea for you. It may mean that you praise God in an unpleasant marital crisis. It may mean praising God in spite of that taxing personal relationship you've had in your marriage for ten years. Perhaps you are troubled and perplexed about your spouse's behavior. That is exactly when God wants you to praise Him.

Where there appear to be no answers, no solutions—and you face an immovable mountain—why not praise Him? What do you have to lose? You have already run out of your own answers. Why not admit it and look elsewhere for solutions with an attitude of acceptance? I have learned to practice what I am suggesting to you. I've not always done this. But for the past several years I have and what a difference it makes, what a comfort it is. I've learned to praise God for being with me in situations, difficulties, roadblocks—and for major decisions in advance.

Dr. Lloyd Ogilvie has an interesting thought along this line: "Consistent praise over a period of time conditions us to receive what the Lord has been waiting patiently to reveal to us or release for us."[4]

We readily thank people after the fact—or if we have a guarantee that they will help us out of a predicament according to our plan. But to put our future in the hands of someone we cannot see or touch and say, "Whatever You bring about in this matter, I praise You," is not typical. We are guarantee-oriented people, not risk-takers. We resist and rebel at the thought of praising God in every situation.

But think about it for awhile before you discount the advice to give thanks "in everything" (1 Thessalonians 5:18). We have read and heard this passage presented dozens of times and perhaps ignored it. But it just sits there and doesn't go away. On occasion, we grasp at it during times of panic. But what if this principle of praise became as regular as our daily eating? What might happen to us? It is worth a try. Why? This is the better way!

When you and I rejoice in the Lord, we do not do it because we feel like it. It is an act of will, a commitment. Isn't that what it takes for a marriage to make it today! When we rejoice in the Lord, we begin to see life from another point of view. Praise is our means of gaining a new perspective and new guidance for our bogged-down lives. You may be thinking that you are too busy during the day to stop and praise God. That is just the time to do it, when you are to busy, fretful and overwhelmed. When your mind is cluttered with concerns over your marriage, stop, clear your mind and praise God. You will feel refreshed.

Praising God in advance of a solution is an act of faith, a way of saying, "I don't know the outcome, but I am willing to trust."

> Praising the Lord makes us willing and releases our imaginations to be used by Him to form the picture of what He is seeking to accomplish. A resistant will makes us very

uncreative and lacking in adventuresome vision in the use of our capacity of imagination. God wants to use our imagination in the painting of the picture of what He is leading us to dare to hope for and expect. We become what we envision under the Spirit's guidance. That's why our own image of ourselves, other people, our goals, and our projects all need the inspiration of our imagination. However, until the Holy Spirit begins His work releasing it, our will keeps our imagination stunted and immature.[5]

The *third element* involved in this process of changing our lives is encountering the Word of God in a radical new way. For some, the words of Scripture may not be new, for others it might be—but knowing it and practicing it are two different things!

There are three steps involved in this third element. The first is *memorize the Word of God.* Since our thought life is such a critical factor in how we respond to others and to ourselves, we need a radical reconstruction. Charles Swindoll describes it in this way:

> In order for old defeating thoughts to be invaded, conquered, and replaced by new, victorious ones, a process of reconstruction must transpire. The best place I know to begin this process of mental cleansing is with the all-important discipline of memorizing Scripture. I realize it doesn't sound very sophisticated or intellectual, but God's Book is full of powerful ammunition! And dislodging negative and demoralizing thoughts requires aggressive action. I sometimes refer to it as mental assault.[6]

The verses I would suggest have to do with your relationship with your spouse (as well as others). What would happen if we acted upon or reflected these passages within our marriage (and these are just a few!)?

Romans 12:15,16 "Rejoice with those who rejoice, and weep with those who weep. Be of the same mind toward one another; do not be haughty in mind, but associate with the lowly. Do not be wise in your own estimation."

Proverbs 14:29 "He who is slow to anger has great understanding, But he who is quick-tempered exalts folly."

Proverbs 15:1 "A gentle answer turns away wrath, But a harsh word stirs up anger."

Proverbs 15:18 "A hot-tempered man stirs up strife, But the slow to anger pacifies contention."

Proverbs 17:9 "He who covers a transgression seeks love, but he who repeats a matter separates intimate friends."

Proverbs 19:11 "A man's discretion makes him slow to anger, and it is his glory to overlook a transgression."

Proverbs 20:3 "Keeping away from strife is an honor for a man, But any fool will quarrel."

Proverbs 25:11 "Like apples of gold in settings of silver Is a word spoken in right circumstances."

Ephesians 4:2 "With all humility and gentleness, with patience, showing forbearance to one another in love."

Ephesians 4:26 "Be angry, and yet do not sin; do not let the sun go down on your anger."

Ephesians 4:29 "Let no unwholesome word proceed from your mouth, but only such a word as is good for edification according to the need of the moment, that it may give grace to those who hear."

Ephesians 4:31 "Let all bitterness and wrath and anger and clamor and slander be put away from you, along with all malice."

Ephesians 4:32 "And be kind to one another, tender-hearted, forgiving each other, just as God in Christ also has forgiven you."

Philippians 2:2–4 "Make my joy complete, be being of the same mind, maintaining the same love, united in spirit, intent on one purpose. Do nothing from selfishness or empty conceit, but with humility of mind let each of you regard one another as more important than himself; do not merely look out for your own personal interests, but also for the interest of others."

Colossians 3:13 "Bearing with one another, and forgiving each other, whoever has a complaint against any one; just as the Lord forgave you, so also should you."

Perhaps that sounds like too many verses. You don't have to memorize them overnight. When I was at Westmont College many years ago, a chapel speaker said if we would read a chapter of the Bible each morning and each evening for a month, that chapter would be ours for life. It's true. It works once it is within you. The Holy Spirit can bring it to your awareness at the appropriate time.

The next step is to *apply the scripture to your life* and your own situation. Ask yourself the question, "If I were to put this passage into practice today with my spouse, how would I do it?" That's a good question. How *would* you apply each of those passages in your relationship with your spouse?

This leads to the third step of *visualization* which again is best described by Charles Swindoll:

> Perhaps the best single-word picture is *visualize.* Those who break through the "mediocrity barrier" mentally visualize being on a higher plane. Then once they "see it," they begin to believe it and behave like it. People who soar are those who refuse to sit back, sigh, and wish things would change. They neither complain of their lot nor passively dream of some distant ship coming in. Rather, they *visualize* in their minds that they are not quitters; they will not allow life's circumstances to push them down and hold them under.[7]

Imagination is a creative function within us. It's the way we see things. It's true we vary in how much we use our imaginations and the way in which we use them. But we all use the imagination to some degree.

Our minds can create images so realistic they chart the direction we choose to move, for our actions and feelings begin there. Imagination can be used to bring about the positive changes we seek in our lives. Sometimes we call this *visualizing* or *imaging.* When you think of responding to your spouse in a negative way, this is imaging. When you think of responding to your spouse in a positive way, this is imaging. You have a picture in your mind of what you either want to do or plan to do. This is what keeps so many couples from improving their marriages—an inability to visualize a better relationship.

For change and growth to occur, a person must both creatively imagine and specifically define what the new relationship will be like. Without visualizing what you want to be different, how would you know what steps to take? How would you know the direction to move or which goals would be appropriate to select? Do you want a challenge? Take each of the Scripture passages listed above and visualize yourself doing what each passage says in your relationship with your spouse. It can make a major difference. Let's see how.

I've already stated that there are many people today whose first response to the challenges of a hurting marriage is one of these: "I can't do that"; "It's over my head"; or "If I try that, I will fail." This feeling of inferiority limits their efforts and keeps them caged and shackled as the marriage deteriorates. Perhaps you, too, feel inadequate and inferior. God is present in the life of every believer who feels inferior, as well as those who do not. How can you release the power of God within you? What can help you begin to take risks? Perhaps Helen's experience can help you.

Helen was growing more and more frustrated about her husband who was becoming a full-fledged workaholic. Sam was very conscientious about his work but was rarely home. To top it off, he had not taken any vacation time for three years, and vacations were very important to Helen. She felt that she was raising the children by herself. Her attempts to convey her concern to Sam were met by excuses and promises that if she would just be patient for a few more months, he might be able to cut back. But he was in a job where essentially he controlled his own time.

Having seen the destructive results of this pattern in other families, Helen decided that she had to change her approach. Several weeks earlier she had learned the importance of the suggestions given throughout this chapter. She knew that what she had tried hadn't worked. There had to be a better way.

Her thought life was positive and hopeful and she began to focus on scriptures which dealt with the wisdom of God, passages from Proverbs which centered on how to speak and Ephesians 4:15, "Speaking the truth in love." Helen took a piece of paper and outlined several ideas. Then she began to think of how to apply the scriptures. After that she began to visualize what she would try with Sam. Finally she spent time in prayer asking for wisdom and the courage to act.

One day at work, Sam received a telegram requesting his presence that evening for dinner with "one of his most valuable clients." He was told to be at one of the finest restaurants in the city at 6:30 that night. The telegram stated that it was important for him to be there since he was on the verge of losing this important client. Reservations had been made in his name. He was totally befuddled and perplexed and no one he talked to, from fellow workers and secretaries to restaurant personnel, could shed any light on the situation.

He decided that he would go and he did. When he arrived, he was shown to a table and told that the other party would be a few minutes late. A few minutes later, much to his surprise, his wife Helen walked in, smiled and sat down. He about fell out of his chair.

"Did you send the telegram? Are you the client? What is this?" he asked.

"Yes, I did send the telegram and I am the client," she replied. "I need to talk to you. I feel as though I am one of your neglected clients. Because of the past three years, I was wondering when it is that you are planning to drop me out of your life."

Sam was shocked. His next few responses were met with that same question, "When are you planning to drop me out of your life, Sam?"

Finally, he said, "What do you mean? I've never planned to drop you, Helen. I care for you. I need you. I love you. I always want you with me."

"But I don't feel that you want me or need me," Helen replied. "I love you, too, and want our marriage. But I feel as though I'm a stranger to you. I know your work is important. I appreciate your dedication and diligence. Those are wonderful qualities. But I want your time, diligence and dedication for our marriage as well. I want to spend this evening with you. So let's go ahead and order dinner and you can continue to think about what I've said." She opened the menu and then said, "If you would like to talk about how we can build our marriage, I'll listen. But I will not listen to excuses or reasons for not taking action now. I want action and I want you! Let's eat."

Needless to say, Helen did get his attention. Fortunately, her plan worked. In his discussion with her, Sam admitted that her radical approach captured his attention and let him know how serious she was. Not all situations and changes are so radical, but even small changes need the steps Helen followed.

Visualizing, prayer and action—these are the keys. Picture yourself as Helen did, facing some difficult situation, with our Lord standing beside you. He takes the first step forward, then see yourself taking one step to bring yourself up beside Jesus. He takes another step, and you again move up beside Him. Saturate your mind with the image of the presence of God. Visualizing scripture in a practical way in your life can free you from the fear of failure.

Sure, it takes time, work and effort. The Scripture tells us: ". . . Gird up . . . your minds" (1 Peter 1:13).

But it's worth a try! There has to be a better way! And there is! Now, it's *your* choice.

Life-Changers

The better way is . . . be in charge of your changes by allowing Jesus Christ to renew your mind.

Praise Him no matter what!

Encounter the Word of God through memorizing, applying and visualizing!

But the wisdom that comes from heaven is first of all pure and full of quiet gentleness. Then it is peace-loving and courteous. It allows discussion and is willing to yield to others: it is full of mercy and good deeds . . . (James 3:17–18 TLB).

4

There's a Reason for Your Conflicts

It was 9:30 A.M. on a Tuesday morning. My first appointment was scheduled to arrive in just a minute and I looked at the names. It was a new couple whom I had never seen before. They were referred by a pastor from one of the large evangelical churches in the area. The call had come in the day before and since I had a last minute opening, I was able to schedule them. But there had been no opportunity for them to complete the customary preliminary forms which would have given me a great deal of information. We would just have to find out the difficulties during their first session.

Jim and Sandy came in and sat down, a well-dressed middle-aged couple. After a few minutes of casual conversation, I asked, "What brought you to the place of wanting to see a counselor? What are your concerns?"

Jim looked at me, leaned forward and said in a quiet, tense voice, "I want to know just one thing. I've been married to this woman for seventeen years and I can't understand why we've had seventeen years of fighting. Hassle, hassle, hassle. That's all our marriage is—*one big hassle!* We can't agree on anything. I don't have this problem with people at work. We get along great. Now you're the so-called expert. *You* tell me why there's so much conflict in our marriage. Do other people have this many conflicts? Boy, what I would give for some peace and harmony."

Sandy looked up and interrupted at that point to share her

perspective. The next fifteen minutes seemed to escalate into a small scale border war and I felt I was right in the middle of it. They interrupted, raised their voices, made accusations and threw critical barbs back and forth. Finally I raised my voice, interrupted and said, "Thank you!" They stopped and looked at me and then back at one another. "Thank you!" Jim said. "For what?"

"For answering your own question of a few minutes ago. You asked why you have so many conflicts? The last fifteen minutes just exposed the answers. Would you like to know what I heard?"

They both looked at me and Sandy said, "Yes, I would like to hear. We've been trying to figure it out for years. What did you discover?"

I looked at both of them and then said, "You asked for it and here it is. I heard some of the most common issues which create conflicts for the majority of couples. I heard unresolved issues from your past, Sandy. Jim, I heard you sharing concerns about your low sense of worth. You both have unfulfilled needs and expectations. There are some male-female issues which you have not come to grips with. You haven't accepted your personality differences and you are still trying to make the other person into a revised edition of yourself. You engage in some classic power struggles and you keep the conflicts alive by the intense, vicious circles you've built up. Finally, you've never learned to speak the other person's language. Now that's just for openers.

"I don't mean to be overly simplistic, but the bottom line cause for our conflicts is our sinful nature, which leads me to another question. Where is Jesus Christ in the midst of your relationship? Have you invited Him to bring healing to the issues that are creating your conflicts? Many of them are symptoms of these deeper issues."

They looked at each other silently and then back at me, nodding their heads in agreement with what I had just said. I continued:

"You're looking for a marriage of peace and harmony and one that is fulfilling. You've spent seventeen years building negative patterns. That's the bad news. The good news is *you can change.* I don't mean change your personality. Those who make it in marriage are not carbon copies of each other. They are the couples who have learned to take their differences through the process of acceptance, understanding and eventually complementation. Differing from another person is very natural and normal and can add an edge of excitement to a relationship."

You may be wondering if this couple made it. They did. Others have not. Conflicts are signals that we have other issues in our lives which need attention. In marriage, disagreements are inevitable. But conflicts can be creatively managed for positive results if we learn how.

In a conflict the difficulty is not the issue but the people involved. We bring to our conflicts our past as well as our other frustrations and exhaustion. All this confuses the issue. But the confusion is lifted when the person of Jesus Christ is invited into the process.

Prior to identifying conflicts and their causes, let me suggest another life-changing principle. It comes from the Word of God and if applied and practiced, lives will be changed. *Wisdom.* That's it. Plain and simple. Wisdom. Not man's wisdom. Note with me how this wisdom is expressed in a practical manner. "But the wisdom that comes from heaven is first of all pure and full of quiet gentleness. Then it is peace-loving and courteous. It allows discussion and is willing to yield to others: it is full of mercy and good deeds . . ." (James 3:17–18, TLB). What might happen to our conflicts between nations, as well as between couples, if our attitudes and behaviors reflected these qualities?

What causes most conflicts? A major research study from the last decade identified the following categories: problem-solving or decision-making, child-rearing, home labor distribution, relatives and in-laws, money management, expression of affection and outside friendships.

In yet another study women identified the areas of conflict and the areas in which they wanted their husbands to change. An overwhelming number of women want their men to change their communication behavior. This desire dominates the majority of lists and surveys. And the women usually indicate one of three concerns: 1. There is no communication. 2. If there is communication, it all centers on him.

3. Finally, there is communication but the way in which it is presented is unacceptable. This includes yelling, screaming, becoming angry and inconsiderate. The most common request is the desire for *more* communication. Women do not want to have to beg for more sharing. And naturally this is a common source of conflict and pain in a marriage.

I have spent over twenty years seeing such couples and I know it doesn't have to be this way. The lack of emotional content and ability to share is one of the big concerns. In addition, women are upset over the anger which men tend to exhibit and over their choice of noninvolvement as exhibited in the withdrawal pattern.

A second area of concern is the sexual relationship between a man and woman. It is not a request for more sex, but for more preliminary affection and for sensitivity to the woman's response so she too can achieve an orgasm. The absence of intimacy and sensitivity to a woman's sexual needs is usually the major complaint women voice about the sexual behavior of their husbands.

A third area of concern more frequently mentioned is related to time and togetherness in their relationship. Perhaps the problem with insufficient time ties into the lack of common interests. Many couples spend less than thirty minutes a week together doing something just for the two of them.

The lack of intimacy in marriage will usually generate conflict. Women tend to have a greater need for intimacy than do men. And because men do not respond, wives tend to complain about this aspect of marriage more than their husbands do. This was reported by a counselor and researcher, Dr. John Gottman. He suggests that men and women have different approaches to conflict. Women tend to want to resolve disagreements so they can feel closer to their husbands, whereas husbands will do anything to avoid a blowup. Dr. Gottman believes that men have a more physically stressful reaction to marital confrontations than women do. I have checked this out with a number of men (including myself) and find it to be accurate.[1]

A major tension area (which comes as no surprise) is that of money. The two concerns which women have are that their husbands are either too free with money or too frugal. Many women feel their husbands keep too tight a rein on money matters in their relationship. I am amazed at the number of women who have no idea of how much money is brought in, what their income was for the preceding year and so on.

Both free spending and overfrugality are a problem for a woman since so many feel the responsibility for managing the money.

Money is often the number one conflict with numerous couples. Money conflicts in marriage can be a reflection of the power issue. Money has a multitude of meanings to each person. Do you know the significance of money for you? Is it a symbol of trust and security? Is it basically a means of control? Is money a way of receiving or giving nurturance? Is it a means of declaring independence? Is it a status symbol?

In some marriages allowing a spouse free rein with the finances is extremely threatening. Why? Because to many people, money is an expression of their own independence and power. If someone else has access to their money and a different style of handling finances, there is a definite threat!

Control is a key factor since the person with the most money and control over it displays definite power. In their nationwide survey for their book, *American Couples,* sociologists Pepper Schwartz and Philip Blumstein discovered the amount of money a person earns in comparison to his/her partner's income, establishes relative power in their relationship.[2]

Had you ever considered the hidden meaning of nurturance involved in the finances of a couple? There are many men who believe that the way you demonstrate love to your family is by how well you provide for them. They feel this is the appropriate way for a man. Some men still view their ability to give and provide as an important feature of marriage. On the other hand, there are men and women who marry to be taken care of and money is the way this is accomplished. Years ago, many women married to be provided for and looked for a man who could offer financial security and stability. Being supported was the same as being loved.

I remember a couple I knew years ago who reflected this exactly. Ken attempted to demonstrate his love for his family by working long hours to provide for them. His mindset was, "I demonstrate my love by working hard." June, his wife, did not see it in that way, however. Her message was, "Why does he spend so much time at work? If he really loved me he would be here with me and the children!" He felt devalued by her lack of response to his love. It was important to ask him what his expectations were concerning June's display of appreciation. He did indicate that he expected her to be grateful he was a faithful provider, and to thank him for his sacrifices.

June, on the other hand, did not think the same as Ken did. Working did not have the same value for her when it came to an expression of love. She believed love was demonstrated by being together. Her thought was, *I'll try to have you with me no matter what I have to do.* Unfortunately, this included anger, complaining, nagging, crying or other behaviors. I'm not sure this encouraged Ken to spend more time with June. Here again, messages were mixed and confused. There are four possible changes June and Ken might try:

1. Ken can cut down on how much he works. *Behavior change.*
2. June can change her view of his working so hard. *Attitude change.*
3. June can show appreciation for his sacrifice. *Behavior change.*
4. Ken can change his view of her lack of appreciation. *Attitude change.*

Any one of these changes will help the relationship.

Today both men and women tend to be givers and receivers in the money realm. Both want to feel cared for, but some of the worst conflicts come about when their financial situation is such that the available funds deny them this feeling.

Some people use money as a source for their status. They use it to bolster their self-esteem. But money is a very shaky foundation for anyone's self-esteem. The idea of money equaling status may have come from their parents, from a desire to show their parents that they have arrived, or it may be the easiest way to gain recognition and response from others. Using the following questionnaire, evaluate your own feelings about money:

1. Describe how you feel when there is sufficient money available. ____________________
2. Describe how you feel when there isn't sufficient money available. ____________________
____
3. Describe how your spouse feels when there is sufficient money available. ____________________
____
4. Describe how your spouse feels when there isn't sufficient money available. ____________________
____

I. To better understand how you feel about money, let's look back to your childhood. Indicate with a check how you felt about money as you were being raised.

____ I wasn't concerned. I felt there would be enough money for what I wanted.
____ I felt sure that my parents would have sufficient money for what I needed or wanted.
____ I felt I had less money than my friends.
____ I felt that adults place too much importance on money.
____ I was embarrassed by having too much money.
____ I was embarrassed by having too little money.
____ My life would have been a lot different if I had had more money.
____ I felt that marrying someone with money was important.
____ I wanted to have a lot of money when I grew up.

II. How do you think your partner felt about money as a child?

____ Your spouse wasn't concerned. He/she felt there would be enough money for what he/she wanted.
____ Your spouse felt sure that his/her parents would have sufficient money for what he/she needed or wanted.
____ Your spouse felt he/she had less money than his/her friends.
____ Your spouse felt that adults place too much importance on money.
____ Your spouse was embarrassed by having too much money.
____ Your spouse was embarrassed by having too little money.
____ Your spouse's life would have been a lot different if he/she had had more money.

____ Your spouse felt that marrying someone with money was important.
____ Your spouse wanted to have a lot of money when he/she grew up.

III. When we have conflict over money, the reason is:
____ We disagree over what to spend money on.
____ I think my spouse spends too much at a time.
____ My spouse thinks I spend too much.
____ I think my spouse is too frugal.
____ My spouse thinks I'm too frugal.
____ My spouse doesn't let me know in advance about our finances.
____ My spouse doesn't think I share in advance about my money decisions.
____ Our timing for spending is off.
____ Our financial records are not kept up to date.
____ Money means something different to each of us.

IV. Some of our conflicts over money happen because:
____ I don't really trust my spouse with money.
____ My spouse doesn't really trust me with money.
____ I don't feel taken care of by my spouse.
____ My spouse doesn't feel taken care of by me.
____ I don't like being dependent upon my spouse.
____ My spouse doesn't like being dependent upon me.
____ I don't like to give up control over my money.
____ My spouse doesn't like to give up control over his or her money.[3]

The last of the five most frequently desired behavior changes in this survey is an alteration in behavior toward the children. Extremes were found here as in the other areas. Wives were concerned with the man being either too strict or too laid back with the children. These then were the items women mentioned. Which of these reflect your own marital relationship?

What did men give as their response? What behaviors in women bother them to the extent that they would like to see some changes? It was interesting in the research that in general, men were much more reticent to describe desired behavior changes. Women tend to have longer lists of desired changes whereas men usually have one or two changes. And men tended to talk in generalities.

The one behavior above all others that men would like changed is for women to be more "understanding." This was usually reflected in one of three desires: The men wanted their wives to be more responsive to their needs, to appreciate their efforts more, and third, to nag less.

Another change men desired in their wives was in the area of personal habits and appearance. Weight was the most frequently mentioned item and then came dress, and finally smoking and drinking habits.

As with women the area of sexual satisfaction was of concern to men. The men were more concerned with the frequency of sex which was usually a desire for more but sometimes a desire for less.

Concern over behavior toward the children emerged with the men as well as the women. And most of them wanted their wives to be stronger disciplinarians.

Men desired a change in the area of time and interest as did women, but there was a definite difference. Most of the men wanted their wives to have more outside interests. They felt a woman needed outside stimulus in order to bring more interaction into the marital relationship. Overall in this study, men seemed less concerned about changing behavior in their wives than the wives did with their husbands.[4] Which of these reflect your own marital relationship?

This survey is not the last word since we all have our own agenda for discussion and dissension. Many of the issues are minor.

As I have worked with couples in counseling for the past twenty years, I keep hearing three themes which can sum up these issues—needs, wants and expectations. Major conflicts occur because of unmet needs, wants and expectations. Whenever I hear a conflict, I've learned to look deeper for these three. Right now, I'd like you to take a piece of paper and answer the following questions. Your answers may be quite revealing.

—What are your needs in your marriage?
—How much of your needs are being met?

—What are your wants in your marriage?
—How many of your wants are you receiving?
—What are your expectations in your marriage?
—Which of these are being met?

Have you shared with your partner in such a way that he/she fully understands your needs, wants and expectations? Are you sure? The only way to be sure is to ask! And ask for specific responses. If your spouse does not know, instead of blaming him or her for being insensitive or not listening, share your needs, wants and expectations. But remember, what you consider a need may not really be a need. A need is something you have to have. It is an absolute necessity. Many needs are actually wants and it's important to consider where our wants originate.

Expectations are items that you take for granted will occur or be available. Too often couples fail to share their expectations with one another. Yes, there are reasons for every conflict. We can invest all our time and energy discovering the reasons yet never see changes occur. Remember Jim and Sandy? They made it. Why? They identified the reasons but went on to discover and apply solutions. They also allowed Jesus Christ to have a part in changing their lives. Let's move on to discover more life-changing principles.

Life-Changers

Identify the deeper reason for your conflicts.

Discover and share openly your needs, wants and expectations.

Allow discussion, be willing to yield, be full of mercy and good deeds.

Let the peace of Christ rule in your hearts, to which indeed you were called in one body (Colossians 3:15).

Yes, There Are Solutions!

Several years ago, a friend reintroduced me to puzzles. Several decades had passed since I had encountered this challenge. I sat at a table with five hundred pieces of a scene mixed up with no apparent solution. Attempting to make sense of the jumble in front of me began to tax my patience. I couldn't find the right pieces nor could I visualize the solution. I just saw it as a problem and proceeded to rush and ultimately tried to force some of the pieces to fit. They didn't.

Conflict is nothing more than a mismanaged problem. It occurs when we use defective communication patterns and problem-solving approaches. Conflicts are like a puzzle and we need to cautiously select the right pieces and place them carefully together. Soon a beautiful picture develops and in the case of a conflict, the picture is peace and harmony.

There are several principles which must be followed in a marital relationship if you are going to deal constructively with your conflicts and differences. First of all, each of you needs to be intellectually *and* emotionally aware of the existing problems. If one partner is aware both emotionally and intellectually and the other is aware just intellectually, this creates a new conflict. We must understand the emotional impact, or the lack of it, in order to understand one another.

The second principle is "No blame." Do not blame anyone including your partner, yourself, your or his relatives—or God. This may be difficult, but blaming usually involves attacking and the result is additional conflict.

The third principle is that time will not automatically take care of the problems. All time will do to an unfaced problem is feed it so that it soon takes on gigantic proportions! Problems don't go away. They may get buried but they rise again with greater force. Rather than blame and point the finger at who's wrong, it's better to work on *making your marriage what you want it to be.*

The fourth principle is: Be a winner—Don't try to win! When a spouse has a compelling drive to win an argument, discussion or conflict, the war becomes dirty. Some would toss aside the international rules of war to be the victor. I have seen some individuals actually use irrational tactics to win a conflict. These have included throwing up to prove one too sick to go someplace, to becoming hysterical and irrational. Others will purposely wound their partner with a verbal dart when the spouse is vulnerable and hurting. Others raise past failures to make their point, or become a martyr to activate a guilt response which will bring their partner to their point of view.

There is a verse I would like you to integrate into your heart and life. Read it over each day until it is memorized: "Let the peace of Christ rule in your heart, since as members of one body you were called to peace" (Colossians 3:15 NIV). In this verse, the word "rule" implies umpiring. Jesus Christ is acting as an umpire in our hearts. The peace of Jesus Christ is to be the ruler, the decision-maker and the umpire in our lives and in difficulties between couples.

Conflicts in marriage are like crises. Some are totally unexpected and unpredictable—and others are quite predictable. The normal family life cycle is loaded with conflict material from the day of marriage to death. There are normal events—such as the birth of the first child, adjusting to being parents, having teenagers, mid-life transition and the empty nest—that require normal adjustments. But to these you can also add the unexpected crises such as financial failure, a handicapped child, a job promotion which means being gone 110 days a year traveling, loss of a job, a spouse deciding to quit work and go back to school, an aged parent having to live with you and so on.

The factor of timing becomes an issue for many couples as they attempt to deal with marital adjustments. We all have different internal clocks within us. Some of us use a calendar to tell time and others a stop watch. Often these two people marry each other. The wife needs ten minutes to get ready, her spouse needs an hour. The husband wolfs his food, his spouse chews each bite five times. One spouse tells a story in three minutes and the other takes ten to tell the same story.

The way people approach problems and attempt to solve them can also become an issue in a marriage. Some individuals are leapers and others are lookers. Leapers do look, but it's usually back over their shoulders after a decision is made. This has often been called the Intuitive Approach whereby a solution just "leaps into a person's mind." Rarely are the answers totally correct, but neither are they totally wrong. Leapers tend to rely upon past experiences to make their quick formulation of an answer to a problem.

Then we have the lookers. They are the calculators. These are the people who tend to do things "by the book." They look at a problem, identify the elements in it and then come up with a solution. And they often tell you that both their approach *and* their solution is right. And guess what. They are right most of the time! This really frustrates the leapers. But the lookers need all the available data for their decision to be correct.

Both approaches have strengths and advantages. If you need a quick decision in an area that is not all that important, the leaper is the best one to decide. But when you have a problem that is quite important and you need all the facts, the looker is the best approach.

What are you? Do you leap or look? What is your spouse? Is this an area of conflict with neither of you really understanding the other's style of problem-solving? Or have you learned to work together to complement one another? That's the name of the game—learning to complement each other and using your differences together with instead of against each other.

Time becomes an issue in the conflict over career and work. How much time should be given to work and how much for family and home? I have seen numerous husbands who were very upset when their wife worked because she was no longer around to do what she used to do. And now some of that work falls on the husband's shoulders.

All too often, however, the wife ends up with a two-career

job—a position outside the home and one inside because her spouse does not cooperate.

Some spouses are totally absorbed with their work. "I do it all for you," they say. Or, "I have to in order to get ahead. If I don't, they'll get someone else who will."

There is a difference between dedication to work and obsession.

Obsession involves allowing the job to possess and dominate one, and it usually includes using work to avoid some other area of life. Some people use work to create a distance from others and avoid intimacy. Their work becomes a symptom of deeper issues.

When our work becomes the source for our self-esteem and identity, it is highly detrimental to our relationship with others, ourselves and with God. It is a false basis upon which to build identity and self-worth for when the work goes, so do the results it has been feeding. Both identity and self-esteem have their roots in who God is and how He perceives us. And both are a gift from Him and nothing that can be earned.

Is there conflict over work in your marriage? Let's take a look. Check any statements that apply:

____ I like the amount of time I spend at work.
____ I dislike the amount of time I spend at work.
____ My spouse thinks I spend too much time working.
____ I think my spouse spends too much time working.
____ I would like my spouse to do better at work.
____ My spouse would like me to do better at work.
____ I know very little about what my spouse does at work or his job.
____ My spouse knows very little about what I do at work or my job.
____ My spouse would like to know more about my work.
____ I would like to know more about my spouse's work.
____ I would like my spouse to know how I feel about work.
____ My spouse would like me to know more about how he/she feels about work.
____ Sometimes I think my spouse uses work to avoid issues at home.
____ There is no problem between my work and our marriage.

____ There is no problem between my spouse's work and our marriage.[1]

Differences abound in any marriage and they can be divided into two types. The first includes those that can't be helped, such as age, race, looks, home and cultural background. Your personal body metabolism will affect where you want the temperature in the home, whether you wake up bright and eager, ready to face the day, or whether you need an hour to get both eyes focusing. These differences cannot be changed.

But the other type of difference involves those which can be changed. These can include personal habits in the bathroom or at the dinner table, whether you *like* to get up early and your spouse *enjoys* sleeping late or whether one *likes* going out three nights a week and the other *prefers* watching television at home. I'm amazed at how small, learned behaviors, such as having the bedcovers tucked in rather than having them loose, or eating a TV dinner rather than a four-course dinner on a tablecloth, become such major issues in marriage. (More will be said about personality differences in the next chapter.)

One of the reasons differences become such a source of conflict is that they don't match up to the expectations we have when we enter marriage. We touched on this issue briefly in the previous chapter. When couples marry, each brings to the marriage a list of conscious and unconscious expectations which they believe will be met. Each partner enters into marriage assuming that certain events will transpire just the way he or she imagines them and that the partner is going to respond a certain way:

"We will visit my parents each year on vacation."

"My spouse will be home early each evening."

"My wife will not work while our children are preschoolers."

"My spouse will be neat and not leave things around the house."

"We will eat breakfast and dinner together every day."

"We will spend time together each evening talking and making love."

I've always liked what Philip Yancy said in his helpful book, *After the Wedding*. He feels that one of the reasons for the sudden drop in marital satisfaction reported in all the marital surveys concerns adjustments to the daily areas of living and disappointments with the other person's differences. He writes:

> Why can't couples predict adjustments before they get married? We've already seen that their romantic perspectives often blind them. Also, there are adjustments in habits they would not know about before marriage (he tosses and turns at night; she hangs pantyhose in the bathroom; he throws tools into messy, disorganized drawers). These can usually be worked out by compromise.
>
> The real tough problems of adjustment come when partners have different expectations about marriage. What if a wife is used to big birthday celebrations and elaborate Christmas decorations and the husband isn't? What about a husband who expects a seductive, affectionate wife who will hang on him publicly—and finds she's physically aloof? Though hints of these differences appear in courtship, often the huge gulf does not yawn open until after marriage, when the two are thrust together for 16 hours a day, not just when they want to be together.
>
> Does the husband expect the wife to forfeit a career to be a housewife and mother? Does the wife expect the husband to be a career climber? Does the wife expect the husband to keep a well-running, clean car? Who should clean the garage? Who is to take the initiative in sex? If your expectations differ, conflict will result.[2]

Often we fail to evaluate our own expectations and, in many cases, fail to share them with our partner. Unfulfilled expectations generate frustration which leads to anger. This in turn leads to a demand. Demands elicit defensiveness and noncompliance and the loving couple turns into weary wranglers!

When we want change to occur and it doesn't, the law of expectations takes over. Numerous conflicts in marriage are nurtured and fed because of this law. What is it? Simply this: The way you think about a situation (such as the way you expect it to turn out) will determine how you behave in that situation.

If you expect an event will turn out in a positive way, you will probably approach it with a positive attitude and confidence. The way you stand, carry yourself and speak will reflect your attitude. Others will notice your attitude and tend to be influenced by the way you present yourself.

If you are fearful or negative about a situation, unconsciously you will approach it so that you will tend to bring about the very thing you do not want. You will give off signals by showing discomfort, negativism and even awkwardness. One's tone of voice, facial expression and even speech may send out negative signals and these will be read by your spouse. Your belief that your partner will never change reinforces the possibility that he or she will not change. But when you have a positive attitude or expectancy, you are more inclined to take a risk and try something you have never tried before, even though you don't have a guarantee of success.

How do you develop a positive attitude? Simply by behaving as if the new behavior is going to work. Yes, this does mean that you will have to act counter to the way you feel. Fortunately we are able to do this. If we waited around for our feelings to change, would some of us ever take any risks? Some changes will occur exactly the way you wanted and some will be different. That which is most likely to change in a relationship is you! Your own personal changes can effect change in the relationship which in turn makes it highly possible that your spouse will change also!

What can you do to handle the differences that are causing problems between you and your partner? The initial step involves looking objectively at what is happening. I use the word "objectively" because we all have a tendency to cloud the issues.

Listed below are some questions to help you come to grips with your expectations. Try to answer these questions as though you were a third party standing outside the relationship looking in and making your observations. For any phases of a marriage it is important to take time to think (Proverbs 15:28), ask God for insight and wisdom (Proverbs 3:5–7) and respond in writing. It is one thing to think our thoughts in the mind, but it makes such a difference to see them clearly written out. The process of writing gives clarity and also serves to help drain off any emotion that may be festering within us.

The ideal would be for both of you to answer these questions separately and then come together. Sit face to face, holding hands, and share your responses. Touching is a great way to keep a lid on the emotions. As you share, try to reflect back to your partner what you heard him or her say before you give your response. "If I understand you correctly, Jim, you are saying you feel . . . ." Listening must occur first as Proverbs 18:13 says it so well, "He who answers a matter before he has the facts, it is folly and shame to him" (AMP).

1a. What concerns or bothers you the most about your partner? Please be specific. (Example: I like to be on time and my spouse is always late.)

____

____

1b. What is the expectation of your partner that is not being met? (Example: I just assumed that he would learn to be on time after we got married. I expected him to realize that being late creates problems.)

____

____

1c. What is the real reason that this bothers you? (Example: I don't like being late and often he makes me late. It makes me look bad. I want to appear responsible and I don't like to waste time. Besides, if he cared for me, he would make some effort to change.)

____

____

2. What is it that your partner could do about your concern that would satisfy you? Do you want to see some effort, a 50% change or a 100% change? (Example: I guess I would like him to acknowledge that being late is a problem and isn't the best way to live. I would be satisfied if I could see some progress like a 10–20% improvement each week. Is that asking too much?)

____

____

3. What might you be doing that is keeping your spouse from doing what you want him or her to do? Is there any possible

way that you might actually be helping to bring about the behavior that you dislike? (Example: Perhaps he doesn't like my anger or some of my comments about his irresponsibility.)

---

4. What do you think you might be able to do that would be more effective? (Example: I could sit down with him and calmly ask him how he feels about my compulsion to be on time. Perhaps that bugs him. I could ask him if he could be on time for church on Sunday and our Thursday evening date night. Perhaps I could ask him gently what he will do to make it happen and share with him that I really don't want to be the timekeeper.)

5a. Now we begin to meddle! What bothers your partner most about what you do? Be as honest and specific as you can. (Example: My spouse would like me to be less intense and perfectionistic. And I'm sure he'd like me to back off on the time thing.)

5b. What do you think is your spouse's expectation that isn't being met? (Example: Not really sure. Maybe he thought I would be more accepting, or not expect him to be like me or to let a little clutter happen around home instead of insisting the house be spotless.)

5c. What do you feel is the reason your spouse is bothered by this? (Example: Maybe he doesn't think I care about him as much as the house or having everything just right. Perhaps I need to ask him to find out!)

---

6. What could you do in regard to your partner's complaints to make him/her happier? (Example: I could back off on some of my demands around the house or not expect him

to be like me so much. Perhaps I need to affirm and encourage him as a person a lot more.) ______________

7. What might your partner be doing that makes it difficult for you to change? (Example: When he withdraws or pouts, I get ticked and don't want to change. I would rather he be clear and straight in what he wants from me.)

8. What could he or she do to be more effective in helping you change your behavior? (Example: I would like to have him make requests of me. I would like him to cooperate with me when I do want the house neat and encourage me for my efforts instead of calling me "Mrs. Clean" or the "White Tornado!")

9. Which of your expectations for your spouse are unrealistic or perhaps impossible to attain? (Example: I guess it's not reasonable for me to expect that he will be on time all the time. Perhaps I could identify those times that are vital and let some others go.)

10. Which of your partner's expectations for you are unrealistic or too difficult for you to attain? (Example: I think I will always like things neat so that won't change. I will always be a perfectionist so I'm not sure. Maybe he has other expectations that I'm not aware of and I need to ask him to think about it and make me a list and see what is going on inside of him.)

11. Now list several expectations that you have met for your spouse and several that your spouse has met for you. State when the last time was that you shared your appreciation for these behaviors with your partner.[3]

May I share a warning with you at this point? The next suggestion may sound a bit radical, will involve considerable thought and time, and if implemented, will dramatically affect your conflicts. I want you to be forewarned since change involves time, energy and work. But be thankful! There is hope and for this you can rejoice! Read on.

During the fall of each year an addictive phenomenon occurs. Millions of people become possessed by twenty-two men running up and down a hundred-yard striped field on Saturdays, Sundays and Monday nights. Television sets are fixed on those channels depicting such mania. Football has arrived. When the game is over fans discuss and rehash the events of the game and then wait for the next one. But the members of the football team, whether they won or lost, do a complete play-by-play analysis of the game. This includes viewing each play, often more than once. The plays on the offense and defense are analyzed, evaluated and critiqued very carefully. Why? To learn from their experience and do better the next time. That sounds sensible.

Do you do the same after a disagreement or a conflict? Is there a debriefing on your part or together? If not, why? This is a prime time for you to evaluate what happened and how you reacted following the encounter and make the necessary changes before the next experience.

I'm going to suggest that you consider doing an after-the-fact analysis in writing. If each of you could complete this in writing, and then share the results, what a learning experience it could become! Yes, I will admit that the suggestions which will be given here take time. But as I often ask clients who say they are busy and have too much already going on in their lives, "*How much is your marriage worth?*" If you are committed to staying together and fulfilling your commitment before the Lord, then you need to put forth time and energy to learn new constructive ways of responding to one another which will bring harmony and satisfaction, and be glorifying to the Lord.

Now, let's return to your video replay and debriefing. It's important that both of you respond to this exercise, but even if your spouse won't, you will learn through this activity.

Following a conflict, keep a Conflict Growth Booklet. List your response to the following questions and keep it handy for twelve hours following the conflict. You will be returning to the booklet throughout the day as thoughts and feelings arise.

During the Conflict

What negative feelings did you experience?

What positive feelings did you experience?

Did you express these feelings during the conflict? How?
  Verbally—
  Non-verbally—

After the Conflict

Describe the thoughts that you have toward your partner.

From your point of view, what was the conflict about?

From your spouse's point of view, what was it about?

What did you say to contribute to the conflict?

What did you want to say but never did?

What were you hoping to avoid?

What was your spouse hoping to avoid?

List the excuses you heard from either of you.

List the accusations that you remember.

Was this a separate distinct problem from others or is it connected? To what other problems do you feel it is connected?

List two or three areas of disagreement in your conflict.

List two or three areas of agreement in the conflict.

As you reflect back, what outcome did you want?

What did you regret about the encounter? Describe in detail and then describe what you could have done differently.

Have you experienced anger or resentment toward your partner? If so, what did you want to do to get back at your spouse?

Have you talked to your spouse about the conflict after it occurred?

If so, what were each of you attempting to accomplish? What did you want from your partner?

Did anyone use silence? If so, what did it accomplish?

What was left unspoken? What could have been left unspoken?

What positive thoughts have you had for your spouse?

What romantic thoughts have you had?

Have their been any romantic approaches since the conflict? If so, was it too soon or soon enough for you? What about your spouse?

How often have you thought about the conflict?[4]

The Next Day

Honest sharing after the conflict can result in growth. The *greatest* growth will occur when both of you agree to participate in this new venture. I was able to motivate a couple one day to participate in similar homework exercises by asking the somewhat resistant husband if he knew what he had spent on marriage counseling up to this point. He didn't. I was amazed at his change of heart and agreement to put forth the time and effort when I pointed out he had already paid out $2400.00 for counseling.

The suggestions in this book can be applied by a couple on their own, thus saving what they would pay for counseling. But some couples develop such conflictual patterns that they need a third party. In that case, going for counseling is a wise step. But it is essential that you find a counselor who will require homework and promote growth on your part so you don't have to continue going for years and years. However, many couples will have the ability to become their own counselors and apply these guidelines by themselves.

How do you share what you've written? Make an appointment and set aside time, whether it be forty-five minutes or an hour. Make sure there are no interruptions.

The first step is to read aloud the following passages of scripture from the Amplified Bible:

He who answers a matter before he hears the facts, it is folly and shame to him (Proverbs 18:13).

He who covers his transgressions will not prosper, but whoever confesses and forsakes his sins shall obtain mercy. He who rebukes a man shall afterward find more favor than he who flatters with the tongue (Proverbs 28:13, 23).

A word fitly spoken and in due season is like apples of gold in a setting of silver (Proverbs 25:11).

He who being often reproved hardens his neck, shall suddenly be destroyed, and that without remedy (Proverbs 29:1).

Hold hands and either pray silently or aloud, asking for the presence of Jesus Christ to be with you in your discussion.

Now share what you have written with your spouse. As you read, your spouse's task is to listen, consider, reflect and not interrupt. When you've each completed reading your reflections, take turns answering the questions below. This is similar to the analysis following a game when the replays have been presented and now the commentary or analysis is occurring. Keep in mind that you are sharing with the person you love and the one to whom you've made a commitment for life:

1. How do you feel about the way you reacted? About the way your spouse reacted?
2. Do you still feel the way you felt during the conflict? During the twelve hours following?
3. Are you resentful toward what your partner did or embarrassed by what you did or said during the conflict?
4. Do you feel you are remembering what occurred realistically? How would your spouse describe what happened?
5. Describe for your spouse what you remember happening using two versions:
   a. Describe it from an emotional perspective (your feelings).
   b. Describe it from a factual perspective.
6. Have you fully faced your hurt or anger and feelings of distance?
7. What did you learn from your spouse's presentation? Be sure to share your response from a positive perspective.

8. Describe how you see your partner dealing with conflicts.
9. Ask your partner, "What else would you like me to share about the conflict?"
10. Describe what responses and behaviors you would do differently the next time. Describe what you would be willing to give at this time to resolve the conflict.
11. What will you do the next time to make it easier on yourself and your spouse?
12. Share with your partner how you feel this type of discussion helps your relationship.[5]

If you are a brave couple, the next suggestion is for you. But it is not for the faint-hearted. For years I have asked couples to use tape recorders at home. I suggest that they tape their discussions and conflicts. And naturally I've heard many excuses as to why this won't work. These include, "If we know it's on, we'll behave differently." Perhaps, but in a few minutes most people forget it's on and resort to their previous behavior.

Others say, "We might be in another room and the recorder isn't there." One wife solved this problem by wearing the recorder around her waist. And this was before the miniature Walkman recorders! But the bottom line is this: If a couple wants to change their style of resolving conflicts, they'll find a way!

What I'm getting to is this: Agree to tape-record your next three disagreements. That's all. You don't have to tape any more than three. But both of you must agree that you will record your interaction. When the conflict is over, wait awhile and then listen to the tape. It may be best for each of you to listen alone while you respond to the questions below. After listening and analyzing what happened, write out the changes that you are going to make. *Do not* list the changes you feel your spouse should make.

The Injury

What are you really fighting about?

Who felt hurt, when and why?

Defending

When did you interrupt?
When were you interrupted?
When did you refuse to listen?
What caused voices to be raised?
When did you ignore what was said?
What editing of your comments did you make because of the tape recorder? Why?
When did you feel trapped and most like running away?

Distorting

How logical did you sound?
How unreasonable did you seem?
When did you sound selfish?
When were you unfair?
When did you bully?
When did you insist on being right?

Telling the Truth

What would you like to take back?
Why did you say it to begin with?
When were you lying?
What feelings or facts did you omit? Why?
When could you have been more direct?
When did you have trouble understanding?
When did you feel misunderstood?

Attacking

Who blamed whom and when?
At what specific point did you get drawn into fighting?
Why did you lose your distance?
What tender spots were touched and when?
How did you provoke your partner?
When were you hurtful?
What led up to your attack?

Retreating

When did you become silent?
What were you feeling and thinking during the silence?
When were you not really listening?
What was it that shut you off?
When did you feel let down?

What compromises did you make to keep the peace?

What positive feelings did you have for your partner during the argument?

Honest answers to these questions will give you new insight into how you argue. Once you have actually heard yourself arguing you will become much more aware of the tactics you use, tactics that may well aggravate the problems between you and your partner rather than solve them.[6]

Life-Changers

Identify, clarify and evaluate your needs, wants and expectations.

Let Jesus Christ rule in your heart!

. . . be of the same (agreeable) mind one with another; live in peace . . . (2 Corinthians 13:11 AMP).

6

You Are Different . . . and There Are Good Reasons!

The car pulled to a halt at the end of a narrow, bumpy road winding through a forest. Before us was a break in the trees through which we could see a wide expanse of Cottonwood Creek in the Grand Tetons National Park. My friend and I got out of the car and soon had on our hip boots and fishing accessories. We started across the stream at the shallowest point we could find. I went much more slowly than I usually do, for this was my friend's first experience at wading through the rushing waters. We paused in the middle of a sand bar and without saying much we both enjoyed the beauty around us. Tall cottonwood and aspen trees abounded; through them we could see the snow-tipped peaks of the Teton range.

Before us lay another segment of the stream through which the water rushed so deep and fast that wading was impossible. One at a time, we walked carefully over a twenty-foot log that spanned the stream. Once across the log, I left my equipment, went back and carried my companion's equipment over. Then I waited as my companion slowly and cautiously inched across the log. I gave silent encouragement and suggestions until the crossing was made. Then we went on, talking, wading through small pools and tributaries, fishing, laughing and sharing.

Wild flowers were everywhere—paintbrush, columbine, balsamroot, blue harebells and lupine. From time to time we would call one another's attention to a new flower that we noticed. We waded through another section of the stream and into a marshland where the water deepened quickly. Since my companion was not as tall as I, the water came very close to the top of the waders, and walking was much more difficult. As we pushed and plunged through this grassy and watery section, my companion held onto my belt in order to follow in my footsteps and avoid a sudden drop-off.

Breaking clear of this portion of the river, we were faced with water that was clear, but rushing rapidly. I kept on going and looking ahead until I heard a call to stop. My weight and height enabled me to walk through this portion of the stream, but the force of the water was almost too great for my friend. So we tried walking close together and timing our steps. When both of my feet were planted firmly upon the rocky stream bottom, my fishing partner took a step. When my partner's footing was firm, I took a step. As we cooperated and worked together, we made progress. My friend was willing to try a new activity over unfamiliar terrain. I was willing to slow my pace to accommodate another's ability.

As we neared the other side of the stream and I started to climb on top of a log, I looked across at an island thirty feet away and came face to face with a mother moose. I stopped, touched my companion's shoulder and pointed silently. As we watched, a calf ambled to its feet and gave us the onceover. Then mother and calf went back to their leisurely pace of selecting the choicest portions of leaves for morning breakfast. We carefully circled the island, keeping our eyes on the mother moose in particular, and continued our journey down the river. Soon we reached the point where the Cottonwood and Snake rivers joined.

A few hours later we reached our car, physically exhausted, thirsty and hungry. But it had been a time of enjoyment, a time that we would remember. This fishing excursion was a bit different for me. I went more slowly than usual and traveled a shorter distance. I took more time to notice my surroundings instead of spending every moment concentrating upon catching cut-throat trout. It was a new experience for my friend, and I wanted that friend to enjoy what I had been enjoying for many years. This person is very special, for she is my wife.

Because of changes in our family structure, Joyce now has the freedom to take more of these trips with me. I didn't mind changing the style of my fishing trip for the pleasure of having her along. The trip was successful because I accepted my wife's differences and did not demand that she participate with the same intensity nor in the same way that I usually do. This same principle is paramount for harmony within the marriage relationship. You differ, I differ, everyone differs from other people. Thank God we were not all made clones!

Have you ever raised a litter of puppies or kittens? We have. It's a delightful experience. The first time we helped parent five Sheltie puppies (along with their mother) we were novices. As we learned, we marveled at what we saw unfolding each day. The five puppies' personalities began to emerge and soon it was easier to identify each one because of their differences. There was the dominant aggressive pup, the passive hesitant one, the people-pleaser, the one who just ambled through life without a care and the attention-seeker. Sound like some people you know?

If you were to ask me why each one in that same family of Shelties was so different, I really couldn't explain why.

If you were to ask me why people in the same family are so different, I *could* give you some reasons.

Each person is different because of his or her physical make-up, such as metabolism, neurological structure and so on.

Each person is different because, although we may be born into the same family, it's a different family each time a new child comes along. The firstborn has two young parents and together, they make up a trio. The thirdborn has two older, wiser and wearier parents—and is part of a quintet. Birth order *does* account for individual differences.

Each person is different because of his or her unique life experiences and the responses of others which help to shape our personalities.

Men and women have some obvious differences, but are you aware of the unique differences in men's and women's brain structure and what that means?

Do *you* know why you are the way you are? Why your spouse is the way he or she is? Do you understand what each one's unique characteristics are? Are you responding to the other person with acceptance and understanding and learning to work together? It is possible!

Each of the reasons for individual differences blend together to make a unique person "wonderfully made."

"Why are you the way you are?" becomes an overly significant question for many people. It does help to understand the "why," but it's more important to discover, "Because you're a certain way, here is the best way to respond to you." Let's consider these tendencies in people and realize there are uncountable individual differences. The person I describe may be totally opposite from your experience. That's all right too.

Let me describe our first person. We could call him John or Joan. It really doesn't matter whether our person is male or female, but for this exercise we'll call him John. John grew up learning to do things that would meet his parents' approval. He may be an over- or underachiever. Sometimes he does more than he has to do since he often has difficulty deciding when enough is enough. But if he came from a home with overly excessive demands and harsh reactions, he is more likely to underachieve.

It's important for the members in John's original family to adhere to his parents' rules. He often feels quite responsible for his parents. John is usually willing to do more than his share but at times he can be a bit rigid and inflexible. He tends to feel that *his* way is the best.

John tends to be quite sociable and interacts well with others. Even so, being at ease in a social situation is not always easy since he feels that he has to meet the expectations of others. Seeing himself as independent, he is also very goal-oriented and likes to accomplish. Thus, when he talks with others, he has conversations which have a purpose and he reaches decisions that are important. Discussions which stimulate new ideas or produce new information capture his attention. If others around him don't seem to be working together to accomplish something, he might tend to criticize, interrupt, nag or be demanding to get what he wants.

If he feels unrecognized, unimportant—or can't see the purpose for what he is doing—he tends to lose interest. John then seems not to care or else he looks elsewhere for a challenge. He needs recognition and when it doesn't come he may tend to be rebellious, antagonistic or even withdrawn. *Question: How might these tendencies affect a marital relationship?*

John likes to have a complete picture of things, get all the facts and focus on detail when it comes to accomplishing something.

His communication is unique. Verbal description is very important to him. At times he may get nit-picky with "Now, what is the exact meaning of that word?" or "What are the exact facts?"

He responds to feelings through his thoughts. To realize that he has feelings he needs to *think* about his feelings and then to label them. To him feelings are important if they are part of the process of accomplishing a task! (This tendency also applies to women but to a lesser degree. You'll see why later.)

John's sense of self-esteem is built on achievements and how he appears in the eyes of others around him. When he produces and receives recognition, he feels good. His self-esteem is based more on what "he can do" than "who he is," which means he *must* be involved in achieving. Boy, does John become bothered when others critique his performance! If he receives too much criticism, he tends to become discouraged and give up. And when he's threatened he gets angry at the whole world. Withdrawing is the path he takes inside himself. At a time like this he is often fearful and sad, feeling overly responsible for something that didn't go well. His big worry is being abandoned by those who disapprove. He insists that he's right and uses his verbal skills to prove his point.

John is cautious when it comes to developing closeness in a relationship. The capacity is there, but time is essential for it to develop. John risks a little, then waits to see if there's a positive response. Once this is established, he relaxes and responds. *Question: How might John's tendencies affect his relationship with his wife?*

There are times when his fears keep him from developing intimacy with his wife. His biggest concern is being controlled by her. He is hesitant to be vulnerable since that involves the risk of disapproval. And his one tendency to focus on details and facts rather than sharing feelings sometimes blocks intimacy. He wants to be intimate in a "perfect" way. And frequently he talks a bit too much which can inhibit intimacy.

One of his wife's concerns is John's communication. She often feels overwhelmed with his verbosity and details. And she wishes he saw value in other people's "intuition" rather than living life just on the factual plane. One time she says he even tried to change *her* feelings because *he* couldn't find any rational basis for them! She sees him as a person who has a greater need to be right than to express his feelings.

Joan told me that John always wants to be involved in making decisions. And he is good at this. He can sort out the details and make everything very explicit for others. In just about any situation he can list the advantages and disadvantages and gather together considerable information. It's funny though. . . . At times John is more comfortable making minor decisions than major ones. Could it be his fear of the responsibility of a major mistake? Perhaps. But he *is* a real planner and his wife likes this. The problem is, he often doesn't follow through with the steps. It's more like the planning is enjoyable and creative but completing the steps could lead to disapproval and criticism.

Well, that's John. What's the best way for his partner to approach him for harmony and satisfaction in the marriage? If his spouse has *opposite* personality traits and tendencies, his way of relating to life and others could send her up the wall in frustration. Here's what she could do to demonstrate understanding, sensitivity and help create a healthier marriage:

1. Give him explicit recognition for what he does. Share the praise in clear detail.
2. Be sure to give him compliments for "being" as well as "doing." This can help him realize that he is worthwhile just for who he is.
3. Since he tends to forget past accomplishments and pushes to accomplish something new, remind him of what he has done in the past. This will free him to complete some of the detailed work that he might be ignoring as a present task.
4. If he seems to be bogged down in some task and cripples himself with his "detail" tendency, he can be helped by being encouraged to express his feelings of confusion and helplessness at that time. But any hint of judgment and discounting of what he is doing will just bring on an argument.

Asking him questions to help him clarify what he is doing works better than making direct statements or attacks on his performance.

5. Give him plenty of structure. He needs expectations spelled out clearly *in his language* with well defined steps and goals as well.

6. Cooperate with him for he thrives on seeing others follow the rules of the household.

7. If you sense that he feels inadequate, encourage him to share these feelings. If he can learn that others understand these feelings, he will feel relieved. He can learn that it's ok not to be perfect. (He will be helped too by reading *Living with a Perfectionist* by David Stoop, Thomas Nelson.)

8. Be sure to let him know he doesn't have to do everything by himself. Others can assist him and it's all right. It's not a reflection on his ability.

Now, based upon the description of this person which you have just read, list two other possible responses which would help in getting along with John.

9.

10.

Do you know anyone like this? Yourself? Your spouse? Your friends? The world is full of them. Are you ready for a profound statement? Here it is. If a couple has any children at all, whether one or three or eight, they always have one child like John! Brilliant? Not really, for in general terms we are talking about the *firstborn child.* This person is driven by success because he is his parents' first experiment. He (or she) was probably pushed by his parents instead of being allowed to develop at his own pace. They wanted him to sit and stand and walk and be potty-trained at the proper age or even ahead of schedule. These children grow up fast and feel the pressure of the world around them.

Knowing the birth order of a person is helpful in understanding his or her tendencies or, as a friend put it, "their peculiar bent." When he said that I responded with, "Huh! I resemble that remark." I *do* fit many of these same characteristics but with a blend of others. Why? Because I was firstborn for my mom and dad but was raised with an older half brother. Even though I was the second child in the home, my parents both responded to me with encouragement and firstborn expectations.

What happens, though, in a marriage when a firstborn marries a firstborn, secondborn, thirdborn and so on? Does it help to understand each other's tendencies? Very definitely it does. Let's take a look and then consider what happens when (as it often does) a firstborn marries a secondborn.

A secondborn, whether male or female, is often a bit difficult to describe or generalize about. So often, her lifestyle is determined by her perception since she plays off the firstborn. The tendency is to be the opposite of the firstborn. She could be a pleasant pleaser or an antagonistic person, a controller or manipulator, a victim or a martyr.

Secondborns have good emotional antenna. They are able to identify the emotional needs and feelings of others. As they interact with others they tend to be tender, sensitive and caring. Quite often they act on feelings and intuition rather than facts. They pick up subtle messages which others fail to notice.

Since they are usually not as structured as firstborns, secondborns are freer in their interpersonal relationships. They might even ask inappropriate questions, or give too much information. They are often more concerned about getting the job done correctly than a firstborn and focus on the details. In a task setting they will also pick up the emotional undercurrent and respond to that. Often they tend to add stability to a relationship by their tendency to adapt easily to another's style of responding. In the communication process a secondborn individual will tend to zero in more on implicit messages, feelings and process rather than actual content. This can be frustrating if one is married to a person who focuses on the apparent and obvious bottom line content. But don't be surprised if this same person totally responds to feelings at one time and then deals with facts to the exclusion of feelings at yet another time.

Secondborns tend to draw close to others quickly in contrast to the firstborn. Since they are adept at picking up subtle emotional cues, they are alert to the intimacy needs of other people. Their intuition level helps them know what others are experiencing often before the other person is even aware. They are good at sensing but have difficulty translating it clearly into factual statements. They need more assistance from others with intellectual intimacy. It helps if their partner engages them in factual intellectual conversations. They can develop into even better communicators by becoming more explicit verbally and by not assuming that others understand what they know and are thinking.

One of the strengths of secondborns is the ease with which they are able to express warm feelings. Empathy and concern are easy for them to share. However, if they are overloaded with another's emotions, or interact with a person who is emotionally needy, they may become overwhelmed and retreat in fear.

Secondborns can make decisions well as long as there is no confusion about what is expected. They need *clarity.* They can pick up that something may not be quite right with a decision,but may have difficulty figuring out what it is. They like to be involved in planning and can be good at working out the details. They are less task-oriented than the firstborn and will do better working with a number of people. Why? Because they want others to know clearly what is expected and will respond to the feelings of others.

What happens if a first- and a secondborn marry? It happens so frequently. Since both have the ability to talk about facts, this level of communication functions well. They can both communicate on thoughts, interpretations and ideas. Sometimes, though, when a secondborn is responding emotionally, and the firstborn factually, they talk past one another. Firstborns can help their partners when they are too engrossed in emotions. Secondborns can encourage their partners to become aware of the emotional side of life which they tend to overlook. Sometimes firstborns become so involved and independent in what they are doing, their spouses may feel rejected and left out.

Firstborns do well in a marriage when their partner confirms that they do their tasks well. They also appreciate knowing that they do well in social situations. It is important for secondborns to make sure their messages, expressions of encouragement and approval are crystal clear and obvious. Firstborns don't do well with subtleties.

A secondborn spouse needs to know his partner values him and that he is important in the marital relationship. Both obvious and subtle messages get through to the secondborn.

Both first- and secondborns tend to feel responsible for their original families. This could cause difficulties within the marriage. Secondborns tend to bring more unresolved emotional issues with them into their marriages. If these issues continue unresolved they may begin to resurface in the marriage.[1]

Wow! Isn't life and marriage complicated? Well, not really, but we tend to make it that way. If we all understood a bit more about ourselves and our place in our original family, it would be easier. I've just given you a simple overview of the first- and secondborn to illustrate their uniqueness and the importance of these factors in a marriage. For those of you who are third, fourth or even further down the line, I am not neglecting you nor is your position any less important. Space dictates what can be shared. But no matter what your birth order position, I would encourage you to read *The Birth Order Book* by Kevin Leman and *No Two Alike* by Barbara Sullivan (Fleming H. Revell).

To help you adjust and complement each other in your marriage, do the following. Make a list of your characteristics and tendencies, then ask your spouse to make his or her own list as he or she perceives you. Ask your partner to complete the same assignment. Then share your lists with one another and discuss the following statements:

1. Identify your own characteristics and those of your partner that you've thanked God for.
2. Attempt to identify why each of you is the way you are. Is it because of:
   a. Birth order?
   b. Male-female differences?
   c. Life experiences?
3. Discuss how you can take your differences and use them for peace and harmony rather than tension and conflict.

Remember, God's Word says,

"Grow in Christ,
Pay attention to what I have said,
Live in *harmony* and *peace"* (2 Corinthians 13:11, TLB).

Life-Changers

Ask God for wisdom and insight to understand and accept and use your differences.

. . . be of the same (agreeable) mind one with another; live in peace . . . (2 Corinthians 13:11 AMP).

7

Differences: Are You a Thinker or a Feeler?

We are all different—mixtures of various tendencies. And those tendencies are neither right nor wrong. The problem arises when one of our tendencies becomes so dominant that our strength becomes a weakness. It fails to allow for alternate ways of responding to life and we become entrenched in our own style and threatened by differences. Remember this: the person who has the greatest flexibility and responds to situations in a variety of ways will derive the most out of life and impact a greater number of people!

What are some of these tendencies which draw us to each other but have such conflict potential?

Some of us are thinkers and some are feelers.
Some of us are savers and some are spenders.
Some of us are amblers and some are scurriers.
Some of us are inner people and some are outer people.
Some of us are bottom line and some are ramblers.

And the list continues. In this chapter and the next we will look at some of these tendencies which may provide you with insights about your spouse, and yes, even about yourself.

Some are thinkers and some are feelers. I'm not saying that the thinker doesn't feel and the feeler doesn't think. But they differ in the importance they give to each of these factors.

Take the thinker, for instance. Some men and women tend to emphasize thinking. They deal methodically with small pieces of information and analyze each part separately and sequentially. The thinker is aware of what he is doing and why. He likes to converse about ideas, facts and concepts. He uses logic and concepts while collecting information about decisions. Lists of pros and cons are important. His is more of a situation-based decision process compared to a people orientation. A thinking man believes he is showing love by working hard, bringing home the check and being a good provider.

Who tends to be the thinkers—men or women? A majority of men incline toward the thinker category. Again, let me emphasize that thinkers *do* use the emotional side of their lives. And there are plenty of men who *are* feelers. But a thinker trusts this approach to life more than emotions and feelings.

Feelers are people who trust their gut reactions, their intuition and their hearts more than their heads. They really don't like having to base what they do on facts and logic. Generally speaking, women tend to be the feelers rather than men do. Many of them tend to handle information more as a whole rather than in small pieces.

Feelers want to appear compassionate, understanding and insightful. More than anything else, they are influenced by people's needs and opinions. And they have a genuine concern for the physical and emotional well-being of others. They have a definite need to help others feel comfortable.

How are feelers influenced? By comments, nonverbal expressions and situations. They want others to like them so they often make decisions which help their popularity but sometimes to the detriment of good logical sense. They do not like to offend people. An example of this is seen in the difficulty feelers have in terminating employees if they are the boss.

Men and women feelers want harmony in their relationships. But this may cause them to accept "blame" or deny their own preference. There is a positive side to feelers, but they often experience hurt feelings quite easily and many times the hurt lingers on. Resentments and hurts are difficult to overcome. There is a heightened sensitivity to criticism. If someone blames them unjustly, the accusation is handled with difficulty. They expect others to be just as concerned and considerate toward them as they are toward others.

Being empathetic with others is one of their strengths. A

balance is needed, however, since they could take on the hurts of others as their own and become overwhelmed.

Whereas a thinker may enjoy debate and arguing, feelers don't.

Whereas thinkers value being right, feelers value being seen as warm and tender and considerate.

When feelers communicate they like to talk about people, feelings and interpersonal relationships. Most of them relish details. But if the thinker withholds information from them they are easily offended. They do tend to be better conversationalists, whether they're introverts or extroverts.

One of the common recurring problems between the thinker and the feeler runs like this: The thinker husband comes home and shares with his feeler wife that their friends had a baby. The wife asks "Oh! What was it? A boy or a girl? How long was it? How much did the baby weigh? How's mother doing? Was John there to assist?"

Her husband looks a bit blank and says, "I don't know. They had a baby. That's all I remember. Isn't that enough?"

No, it isn't enough for the feeler.

At a recent seminar I shared this illustration and two men came up separately and said they had had the same experience. They knew how important it was for their wives to have all the details so they made a point of gathering all the important information (thinkers!). They went home and shared what they had learned. Except that each one of them failed to remember whether the baby was a boy or girl! At least it was a good first try!

One of the most common conflicts and sources of frustration in marriage is the tension between a thinker and a feeler. Over the past twenty years I have conducted marriage seminars across the country and in Canada. One of our activities is a fish-bowl exercise in which we have wives sit in small groups with their husbands sitting behind them. The wives are asked to discuss, "How the communication of the opposite sex frustrates them."

Without exception it is possible to predict what will be shared. The two major issues are: "I wish he shared his emotions with me" and "I wish my husband would share more details with me." Husbands failing to share their feelings is a constant complaint. Some have even thought that men have different emotions than women. This is not true! We are created male and female as emotional beings, but with certain subtle differences which will account for some variations.

I remember talking with one wife who said, "When I talk with my husband, I wish he didn't think he always had to define everything. I feel as if I've been talking to a dictionary. He'll say, 'What do you mean? I can't talk to you if I don't understand your words. Give me some facts, not these feelings.' Well, sometimes I can't give him facts and definitions. Man shall not live by thoughts and definitions alone!"

Another wife shared with me, "I don't think that men understand the difference between sharing their feelings and what they *think* about their feelings. They tend to intellectualize so much of the time. Why do men have to think about how they feel? Just come out with it unedited. He doesn't have to respond like a textbook or edit everything he shares. I wonder if the emotional side of a man is a threat to him? Of course, you can't always control your emotional responses. Well, so what!"

I, too, have had to learn how to share my feelings. Fortunately, this happened fairly early in my adulthood. But the reason it took place was beyond my control. I had such a mixture of feelings churning around inside I had to learn to face them, not fear them—and express them. They were there because of our son Matthew. Today Matthew is in his twenties chronologically. Mentally he is about sixteen months old. He is a profoundly mentally retarded child. Discovering this when he was about a year old brought many changes in our family. But Matthew's condition and presence in our lives brought about growth in a new way for me. I thank God for what Matthew taught me and continues to teach me about patience, appreciation and the joy of life.

Men tend to be like medieval castles of olden days. We erect walls and moats for protection. Why? One reason for limiting emotional expression is our way of staying in control. Men have a driving need to be in charge and they like to decide who can enter into their lives and when. These walls hide hurts, joys, frustrations, fear, guilt, sorrows and . . . even love.

One wife shared, "I live with a portable fortress. He walks around the house with walls on all sides and a 'keep out' sign hung around his neck. I've tried blasting through the walls, digging a tunnel underneath with dynamite, pole-vaulting over the walls and nothing works." Men are more silent about their feelings than women. And many do not even notice that their feelings are there.

There are other reasons why men tend to hide their emotions. (Remember there will be exceptions and many women fall into the thinker category.) Here are some of them:

1. Men hesitate to venture into an unknown area such as sharing feelings. If we don't know how to share or understand our feelings, we feel it's better to avoid them.

2. Men don't usually have a role model of a man who is emotionally close to others and yet reflects strength.

3. A major concern for men is the fear of losing control of our feelings (which to us means losing control of our lives). Many of us are fearful of letting down the wall, which protects the inner sensitive core, and making it vulnerable to criticism.

4. If others around us tend to live on emotions, we may feel that "Somebody has to keep things in line with facts and logic so they don't get out of hand."

5. A man may have the habit of cutting off communication when his feelings are aroused. Old habits are comfortable because they seem to work well. If a wife expresses feelings and her husband's emotions are activated, he may respond by laughing or making cutting remarks to avoid dealing with his own feelings. Part of him may even yearn to express his emotions, but the safety of years of hiding may override the expression.

6. There is a difference between a man's brain and a woman's! That's right. The nature of the brain does have something to do with this area of difference.

If I could look into your brain or you into mine, we would both discover that the brain is divided into left and right hemispheres. The two sides are connected by nerve fibers. Each side has its own tasks and assignments. No only do the two different sides control our movements, they also determine the way we think. Each side is quite specialized.

The left side of your brain is verbal. It controls your language and reading skills, gathers information, and processes it logically in a step-by-step fashion. The left side of your brain wants to keep your life sensible, organized and on schedule.

The thinking pattern of the left side of your brain is positive, analytical, linear, explicit, sequential, verbal, concrete, rational and goal-oriented. We all use both sides of our brains and some individuals are more left-side dominant than others. Have you ever listened to a teacher or minister focus on dry, detailed facts? Because he was inflexible he was annoyed by interruptions to his train of thought and thus would return to the beginning and review after each distraction. He tended to be monotonous and moved step by step through his presentation with little emotional expression. This is the extreme left-brain dominant individual.

But what about the right side of the brain? What does it do? That portion of your brain comes into play when you work a jigsaw puzzle, look at a road map, design a new office, plan a room arrangement, solve a geometrical problem or listen to musical selections on the stereo. The right half of the brain does not process information step by step like the left portion. Instead, it processes patterns of information. It plays host to our emotions. It has been called the intuitive side of the brain. It will link facts together and come up with a concept. It looks at the whole situation and, as though by magic, the solution appears.

While the thinking pattern of the left side of your brain is positive, analytical, linear and so on, the right side is intuitive, spontaneous, emotional, nonverbal, visual, artistic, playful, holistic and physical.

If you listen to a speaker or someone else in a conversation ramble from topic to topic, rely on his own opinion and feelings, become easily led away from the point, leave gaps in his presentation and give the conclusion, use emotional language and hunches—you are in the presence of the extreme right-brain dominant. The left side wants to know, "What's the bottom line?" and the right side travels around the barn a few times to get there.

Is there a genetic right-brain/left-brain difference between men and women? Yes. This is part of the answer to why men and women are the way they are. At birth the cortex of the brain is more highly developed in women than in men. As infants women respond more to the sound of the human voice than do men. Women are left-brain oriented and tend to be more verbally skilled. Men are not. A woman's left brain develops earlier than a man's (this gives her an edge in writing and reading). This is why many little boys do not read or write as well as little girls. A boy can build a complicated model but cannot read as well as the girl who is a year younger. Little boys often become insecure in verbal interaction and are more comfortable with eye/hand games and visual interaction. The male's right brain develops earlier than the female's and all through life men tend to use this side of their brains more skillfully in the spatial area.

A man uses the right side of his brain more efficiently than does a woman. And his brain is more highly specialized. If I am a typical man, I will use the left side of my brain for verbal problems and the right side for spatial. If I am putting together a new barbecue grill which came in pieces, I use my right brain to visualize the end result. Thus I shift from one side to the other. I am seeing how it fits together in my mind. If my wife, Joyce, comes out to discuss who is coming for dinner, I am responding out of my verbal side, the left. But men also tend to shift further left and further right than women.

Personally, I feel that we men do not use all the abilities of the right side as well as we could. The emotional, intuitive side in men is often stunted, partly due to the lack of socialization training and encouragement and partly because of our tendency to use one side of the brain or the other but not so much together.

But a woman is different in the way she uses her brain. And it gives her an advantage over men! A woman's brain is not specialized. It operates wholistically. A man shifts back and forth between the sides of his brain. He can give more focused attention to what he is doing. But a woman uses both sides of her brain simultaneously to work on a problem. The two parts work in cooperation. Why? Because some of the left-brained abilities are duplicated in her right brain and some of the right brain in the left. Women have larger connectors between the two sides even as infants and thus can integrate information more skillfully. They can tune in to everything going on around them. A wife may be handling five hectic activities at one time while her husband is reading a magazine, totally oblivious to the various problems going on right under his nose.

The main reason for these differences is God. He created

our bodies inwardly and outwardly different. He knew what He was doing. Sometimes we fight His handiwork instead of recognizing, accepting and using the differences.

If you are more right-side oriented and your spouse is left-side oriented, how will you communicate? It's as though you each speak a different language! Think about a solution to that problem (if you're right-brain dominant).[1]

The result causes women to be more perceptive about people than men. Women have greater ability to pick up feelings and sense the difference between what people say and what they mean. A woman's expectation of a man's perceptual ability should thus be tempered with such knowledge and a man needs to listen to his wife's hunches more.

Quite often a wife will say to her husband, "Honey, I sense something is going on in that relationship." He'll respond with, "What do you mean? What's going on? I don't see anything. Where's the evidence?" She responds with, "Well, there's no real evidence, but something just doesn't seem right. I just have this funny feeling about it." His response is quite predictable. "Honey, nothing is going on. You're just imagining things. Forget it." And how many times does he later discover her intuitive perception was correct!

This is why a woman may recover some of her functions following a stroke whereas a man remains limited. Her ability to use both sides means that the undamaged side can step in and begin to fill the void left by the other.

Both men and women have a tendency to prefer one side of the brain or the other, and this does affect our approach to life and work. We do not change our preferences or dominance throughout our lifetime, but we can develop the skills of the less-preferred side of our brain. And remember, our culture tends to reinforce these bents and inclination.

Some men store their feelings in an inner file just hoping that the file drawer is closed forever. Others use their wives as a defense against their own feelings. How? Carefully and subtly, they encourage emotional expression on the part of their wives so that they do not have to hear them say, "But we do not share feelings in our relationship!"

Avoidance is often used by threatened men. Situations, events and even people are avoided. I know of some men who are very uncomfortable visiting the home where our retarded son Matthew lives. It's not always comfortable for me either, but those feelings have meaning and purpose. And they can be handled. Men are sometimes terrified by the feeling that they may be losing control and may cry uncontrollably because of the extensive mental and physical retardation they see when they walk onto Matthew's ward.

Many of the men of our day choke up when it comes to sharing tender, caring feelings with others. These men are not cruel, insensitive, noncaring individuals. They just find it difficult to communicate from the inner reservoir of emotional expression. I have talked with such men and I remember one in particular who said, "I was proud of my wife the other day. She's been taking some art lessons and finished her painting. It was displayed in the window of the artist's studio and two people wanted to buy it for an incredible amount of money! I don't know that much about art but I thought it was great and was really feeling good about her success."

I replied, "That's great. How much of what you just shared with me did you tell her?"

He looked at me and said, "Well, I'm sure she knows how proud I am of her."

I replied, "How? How would she know that? Did you tell her what you told me? Did you tell her you were proud of her? Did you tell her you were feeling good about her success? Did you tell her you thought her art was great?"

He waited and thought and then looked up at me and said, "No, I guess I didn't. It would make a difference, wouldn't it?"

"Yes," I replied, "it could change her perception of you to that of a caring person if you would let her in on those inner feelings. They're a tremendous gift which she would like to receive."

As I work with couples in premarital counseling, I administer a battery of helpful tests. One of these indicates whether a person is able to share himself and his emotions in a warm, demonstrative, open manner. If one or both individuals register low on this scale, it is a clear indication of marital discord and dissatisfaction in their future relationship. And if only one is capable of sharing in this manner, the person will end up frustrated and starving for deep intimacy. We may differ in our emotional ability and expression but with the Lord's help we can develop it to become all He wants us to be.

We can learn to be different by allowing Jesus Christ to activate the undeveloped areas of our lives.

To ease your frustration and conflict, remember:

A thinker will never share his feelings exactly the way a feeler would.

A thinker will never share his feelings exactly as a feeler wants him to share. He will share his feelings from a thinker's perspective.

And *that's all right.* In time as each learns the other's way of responding, there will be growth.

If you are a thinker or a feeler, the more intense or extreme you are the more you need your opposite partner. But the more extreme you are, the more threatened you may be by your partner's differences. You may sense your need of your partner's style and how little you really understand him or her. If you feel that way, rejoice! That's your signal that you need what your spouse has to offer. *Listen* to your spouse. A thinker can help a feeler think more precisely. A feeler can help a thinker derive information from emotions and preferences. Take a safari into your spouse's land and see what you can discover. What your partner has to offer is not dangerous nor will you have to give up who you are. You have the opportunity to add a new dimension to your life, gain new insights and discover richer ways of relating to others.

Let's consider where you are. On the scale provided below indicate with an X where you perceive yourself. Use a circle to indicate where you think your spouse falls. Ask your partner to do the same and then discuss your perceptions.

FEELER *THINKER*

1 2 3 4 5 6 7 8 9 10

Now answer the following.

I think (for the Thinkers) or feel (for the Feelers) that I am:

____ % Thinker and ____ % Feeler

My perception of my spouse is

____ % Thinker and ____ % Feeler

If you have a 60%–40% or 70%–30% you have a balance. But when you get to a 80–20 or even 90–10, the greater your need is for your spouse, if your spouse is opposite. One person responded to me with, "What do you mean 90–10! How about 99%–1%! That's how much we differ."

What if both of you are the same—two thinkers or two feelers? Are you comfortable with that? Are there conflicts because of too much similarity? Often there can be. In a case such as this I would encourage you to find friends on the other end of the scale. Learn from them.

"Why?" you ask. "I'm comfortable with the way I am. That's why the friends I have now are the same as myself."

Many people feel this way. But to grow and discover new areas of life that you may not know exist, become adventuresome. I'm not asking you to give up who you are. Try reaching into this new world for awhile until you have fully investigated and explored. Then decide whether you want to remain as you are or continue working on a new way of responding.

This has important ramifications for the business world as well as marriage. Many of the people with whom you have contact fall into different styles of responding. The greater flexibility you have to use their style and speak their language, the greater your influence and the more positive their response to you. (For further information concerning using this approach see Bolton and Bolton, *Social Style/Management Style,* Amacom Publishers.)

Remember God's Word says:

"Grow in Christ,
Pay attention to what I have said.
Live in *harmony* and *peace*" (2 Corinthians 13:11, TLB).

Life-Changers

Accept the thinking and feeling side of you.
Each is God's gift.

Develop a balance and use both for your marriage and for God's glory.

. . . be of the same (agreeable) mind one with another; live in peace . . . (2 Corinthians 13:11 AMP).

How Would You Like to Be Married to Someone Just Like You?

I heard this question from five different couples this week in my office. One couple was engaged, two had been married less than ten years and the other two had been married over twenty-five years. Their remarks and complaints were so similar. Listen to their conversations.

"Why can't you be more outgoing and friendly? You're so reserved."

"Can't you ever settle down? You always want something going on. I need some peace and quiet."

"I can't trust him with a check book or credit card. Spend, spend, spend. We need to think of the future and plan ahead."

"I wouldn't say she's frugal. She's a tightwad. She makes the dollar bleed before she spends it."

"I just love being free and spontaneous. Why plan so much? You're too rigid."

"If we had more organization in our life and identified some goals we'd get somewhere. She doesn't know what I mean by goals. If I didn't plan everything we would really be in a mess. And she wonders why I take charge of so much."

There are many ways in which we differ from one another. One of those ways is in our attitude toward money. Let's consider for a moment the saver and the spender.

A saver is a person who is fairly conservative. He believes

that he might run out of his resources or money so he'd better play it safe. A saver may prefer to stay at home, fix a home-cooked meal, and watch "free" TV than go out and spend all that money at a restaurant and movie theater. Saving for a rainy day and living beneath his means is comfortable for him. He thinks, *I may need this later so I'll hang onto it, just in case.* A saver may even be the pack rat of the family, hesitating to throw out anything. "Who knows when we'll have a need for this?" is a phrase often heard. Isn't it strange how frequently savers and spenders marry?

A spender sees life as having no limits. "Don't worry about the future. Now is the time to live life and enjoy it." Spenders really tune in to the credit card ads which promote the idea of "buy now and pay later." Spenders tend to be quite generous, which is admirable, but they do this even when their resources are dwindling.

Remember that a spender has some of the saver characteristics and the saver has some of the spender characteristics. But they tend to be overshadowed by the dominant tendency. We often fail to give our partner or ourselves credit for having *both* characteristics.

The two tendencies described here can become a major arena of frustration and conflict since each one feels threatened by his or her spouse's way of life. If both husband and wife can evaluate the strengths and weaknesses of their own style and begin to activate their lesser style, they may like what they discover about this other way of responding to life.

If you are a saver or a spender, the more intense or extreme you are, the more you need your opposite partner. But the more extreme, the more threatened you may be by your partner's differences. You may not understand your partner nor sense the need of your spouse's style. If you feel that way, wonderful! That's your signal that you *do* need what your spouse has to offer.

Hear what your spouse has to say. Venture into his or her lifestyle and enjoy the discovery. What your spouse has to offer is not dangerous nor will you have to give up your dominant style. You have an opportunity to add another new dimension to your life and gain new insights.

Let's consider your style. On the scale provided below,

indicate with an X where you perceive yourself. Use an M to indicate where you think your spouse falls. Ask your spouse to do the same and then discuss your perceptions of yourselves and each other.

SAVER *SPENDER*

1 2 3 4 5 6 7 8 9 10

Now answer this question.

I see myself as:

____ % Spender and ____ % Saver

My perception of my spouse is:

____ % Spender and ____ % Saver

If you have a 60%–40% or a 70%–30% you have a balance. But when you get an 80–20 or even a 90–10, the greater your need for your spouse's style (if your spouse is opposite.) What if you are both the same? Consider this: Are you both comfortable being that way? Does it bring harmony or conflict into your relationship? What might happen if one of you begins to drift in the other direction? What might occur if both of you begin to venture into an unexplored land? There may be some new discoveries waiting for you.[1]

". . . be of the same (agreeable) mind one with another; live in peace . . ." (2 Corinthians 13:11 AMP).

Are You an Inner or an Outer Person?

Some of us are inner people and some are outer. Let's consider the inner person. (Remember, the inner person will have some of the characteristics of the outer person. We need a blend of both for balance.)

Inner people tend to live more within themselves than with other people. They think first and then speak. Often they wait to have others respond first with questions, ideas or opinions. They need encouragement to risk sharing what they are thinking or feeling. They are quite cautious about sharing feeling except with someone close and safe. An inner person values privacy and a few people rather than the masses. Privacy and not too much going on at one time gives them a sense of security. Their comfort level goes up when they engage a person on a one-to-one basis.

My wife Joyce is more of an inner person. In a group of people she will listen well to what is occurring between people and then single out one person with whom to carry on a conversation. At home she is very comfortable and we spend a lot of time talking together. She is an excellent communicator but chooses her time and place to share. Speaking in front of a group as I do so much is definitely not in her comfort zone.

In another way Joyce and I fit the pattern of an inner and outer person. When she arises in the morning she likes peace and quiet for a while and enjoys easing quietly into the day. I get up early, bright-eyed and ready to enjoy the early morning. It's all right for each of us to be the way we are. I've learned not to overload her with too much conversation or too many ideas the first thing in the morning. I've learned to pace myself to her level at that time, instead of demanding that Joyce be the way I am. Sometimes inner people like additional time to think over their responses when talking. This is especially true when they are with a group of people. They prefer to wait and share something when it's significant and well thought out.

Many inner people like quiet surroundings. As the noise level increases in intensity, they become uncomfortable. Being around too many people and being with them too long drains them. Their solitude helps them recharge.

Sometimes inner people have a tendency to be a bit pessimistic. Why? Because they tend to internalize their thoughts and feelings. Their cautious natures can keep them from taking risks because they fear that the worst could happen. If they can talk over their inner concerns with others, this tendency is reduced.

An inner person in a marriage adds the strength of being thoughtful, deliberate, thorough and able to contribute some profound thoughts. They don't push themselves into the limelight and would rather wait to be noticed. Inner people take time to build relationships and when this occurs they open up and are quite loyal.

What kind of person am I? I gave you a hint a bit earlier. I am an outer person but as I progressed through my forties I began to discover more and more inner characteristics emerging. This is quite normal, so I've been told. Men in their forties tend to withdraw somewhat and become more thoughtful about themselves and life. The time I spend with people now is highly selective. Socializing just to be with others has been replaced by the value of in-depth relationships with those I really care about.

I've discovered another characteristic about myself. I function and respond often as an outer person when I am with others at seminars and conferences, but away from such situations I am now leaning strongly toward being an inner individual. I've discovered there are degrees of inner and outer.

The true outer person is a talker who exudes energy, confidence and enthusiasm. These individuals do prefer people rather than solitude. They like to have a lot going on and seem to be able to juggle a number of activities at once. They are prone to speak while thinking or in some extreme cases speak first and think second. For some outer people, these passages in Proverbs are essential:

"Don't talk so much. You keep putting your foot in your mouth. Be sensible and turn off the flow!" (Proverbs 10:19 TLB).

"Self-control means controlling the tongue! A quick retort can ruin everything" (Proverbs 13:3 TLB).

"Keep your mouth closed and you'll stay out of trouble" (Proverbs 21:23 TLB).

A true outer person needs people and once in a while privacy. Noise is no problem and often the more the better. Such people make quick decisions and are good jugglers. They can handle many activities at once. Their outlook on life is optimistic. They can handle adversity fairly well and take the approach of "Let's get on with life."

Sometimes outer people share too much and open themselves up to criticism and rejection. Many people believe that all outer people are secure, have high self-esteem and few inner struggles. Wrong! Some are struggling with shyness and insecurity.

Both inner and outer persons can be inwardly secure and at peace with themselves. And both can be equally fearful, insecure, feel inadequate and struggle with life. An inner person would tend to hide this propensity by being quiet, the outer person by being too gregarious and happy.

If you're an outer person, you will look forward to this next evaluation time as you did the others. If you're an inner person you may be hesitant to do so, especially if you have to share it with someone. But let's give it a try.

Remember that the outer person has some of the inner person's characteristics and the inner person has some of the outer person's characteristics. (Have you ever considered that your characteristics are a gift from God? It's something to think about.)

Your lesser characteristics tend to be overshadowed by your dominant tendency. We often fail to give our partner and ourselves credit for having both tendencies. You were drawn to your partner by what you saw and I hope you still feel that way. But for many, conflict emerges because of these differences. If you can evaluate the strengths and weaknesses of each characteristic, and begin to make some slight modifications, you may be able to experience a hidden part of your life.

Whether you are an inner or an outer person, the more intense or extreme you are, the more you need both your (opposite) partner and the more you need to allow your less dominant tendency to emerge. How? By learning from your spouse. You can learn to tolerate a bit more noise or a little silence. You can learn to enjoy a few more "safe" activities or some quiet time.

Let's consider your style. On the scale provided below, indicate with an X where you perceive yourself. Use an M to indicate where you think your spouse falls. Ask your spouse to do the same and then discuss your perceptions of yourselves and each other.

INNER *OUTER*

1 2 3 4 5 6 7 8 9 10

Now answer these questions.

I see myself as:

____ % Inner and ____ % Outer

My perception of my spouse is:

____ % Inner and ____ % Outer

If you have a 60%–40% or a 70%–30% you have a balance. But when you get an 80–20 or even a 90–10, the greater your need for your spouse's style (if your spouse is opposite.) What if you are both the same? Are you both comfortable being that way? Does it bring harmony or conflict into your relationship? What might happen if one of you begins to drift in the other direction?

". . . be of the same (agreeable) mind one with another; live in peace . . ." (2 Corinthians 13:11 AMP).

Are You Organized or Spontaneous?

One of the differences I come across in counseling is the Organized-Spontaneous couple. Spontaneity and organization (or self-control) are admirable characteristics. But often they become extreme and an irritant to the opposite personality. Tensions will ease in a relationship when a healthy respect and acceptance of each person's *balanced* tendency is developed.

Have you ever looked at your spouse's characteristics as a special gift from God? He *did* have a hand in creating us the way we are. Our partner is not the way he or she is just to make life difficult for us. But sometimes (for many reasons) we allow our tendencies to become extreme. Thus, what was healthy and positive may now be negative and detrimental to ourselves and the marriage relationship. That possibility must be faced. Perhaps we can illustrate this possibility by looking at the organized person and the spontaneous person.

Organized individuals enjoy plans. They feel secure by regulating life in a planned and orderly fashion. Some plan not only what they will do tomorrow but next week and next month. An unplanned day is a wasted day. They don't especially enjoy being surprised, although they may enjoy creating and planning a surprise for another person. Life is often lived by a list as well as the clock. Work is far more important than wasting time playing. And when they do play, it has to occur after all the work is done. They love to finish tasks. Many organized individuals end up being driven individuals and some are workaholics.

Organized people respond well to and are encouraged by deadlines. Their appointment book is another extension of their bodies. They enjoy keeping things in order and setting and enforcing rules. For them life is best when it is planned and under control. We need organized people, but many times they become rigid, perfectionistic, full of overly high expectations for themselves and others. They are unable to relax or flex. These extremes make their strength brittle and weak.

An organized person is often drawn to a spontaneous mate because initially he is intrigued by this refreshing, carefree breath of fresh air. But eventually he discovers his partner is much more than he bargained for and must be controlled and changed.

A spontaneous person, on the other hand, likes to adjust to life rather than to organize it. Such people like to see life unfold before them and they resist making plans. "I'm too confined when I have to make plans" is a frequent response. They enjoy fun and excitement. Work should come after fun. As long as they enjoy what is occurring they will keep at it whether it's schoolwork, housework or a job. Spontaneous people work on inspiration. They prefer to start tasks and projects and let others complete them. They often have several projects going at the same time. These tend to drag on without the completion an organized spouse would give to the task. They can handle repetition as long as there is variety. They enjoy meeting life's crises and short-term projects. Their flexibility enables them to meet life's crises better than their counterparts.

Spontaneous people resist control of any sort. They don't mind doing what is right as long as *they* choose to do it. When someone else tells them what to do or attempts to put structure around them, expect some resistance.

The flexibility of this person is a positive quality. But the resistance to structure can create both personal and marital problems such as:

____ Starting housework and not completing it.
____ Starting to remodel the house and taking three years to complete one room.
____ Not planning meals or starting them on time.
____ Being late for appointments.
____ Getting into difficulty because of not considering consequences.
____ Being distracted too easily from one task to another.

What happens when these two people marry? Let me suggest what *not* to do. Don't look at your partner as an enemy or as sick. If you have a struggle with your spouse's tendency it could be either because of the normal tension between opposites or because one or both of you could have moved into the extreme of your tendency. Both of you have so much to offer.

Try responding to life from your opposite's perspective for a week. Radical? Perhaps. You're not giving up your normal way. You're just giving something new a try. Try compromising instead of ending up in a win/lose position or a deadlock. The organized person could lessen the amount and intensity of planning when it involves his or her partner. The spontaneous person could try adding more structure and planning to his or her life.

We often fail to give our partner or ourselves credit for having *both* characteristics. The two tendencies just described can become a major area of frustration. What would I suggest? Evaluate the strengths and weaknesses of this tendency. Endeavor to activate the lesser style.

I'll repeat this statement again: Whether you are an organizer or a spontaneous person, the more intense or extreme you are, the more you need your opposite partner for balance. Remember what I said before about these opposites. Reread the statements about the thinker and the feeler and the others. What was said there applies here.

Let's consider your style. On the scale provided below, indicate with an X where you perceive yourself and use an M to indicate where you think your spouse falls. Ask your partner to do the same and then discuss your perception of yourselves and each other.

ORGANIZER *SPONTANEOUS*

1 2 3 4 5 6 7 8 9 10

Now answer this question.

I see myself as:

____ % Organizer and ____ % Spontaneous

My perception of my spouse is:

____ % Organizer and ____ % Spontaneous

If you have a 60%–40% or a 70%–30% you have a balance. But when you get an 80–20 or even a 90–10, the greater your need for your spouse's style (if your spouse is opposite).[2]

One of the motivating factors which keeps me involved so extensively in premarital counseling is the opportunity to help couples learn about these personality differences well in advance of their lifelong commitment. We assist them in eliminating this surprise element prior to marriage. They will still have to make adjustments but they can face these adjustments with a greater level of understanding and skill. Many upon reading this book did not have that option prior to marriage. Your discovery came as a rude awakening after you married. But it's not too late to understand and adjust.

I have found it helpful to use two tests and a book to assist couples of all ages to learn more about themselves. Let me encourage you to consider this possibility. One of the tests is the Taylor-Johnson Temperament Analysis and the other is the Myers-Briggs Type Indicator. Most counselors and many pastors are aware of these and administer them and share the results with you. I would also suggest you read the book *Self-Esteem: Gift from God* by Ruth McRoberts Ward (Baker Book House). This insightful and practical book deals more with personality differences than self-esteem. Many of my clients have read this book and their perception of themselves and their partner was greatly changed.

I have just scratched the surface in the area of differences. There are many others and countless combinations. You are a blend of these differences with many reasons for them including your sex, environment, family background, birth order and God's creative hand in your life.

Your differences will always exist. The challenge is: What will you do with them to build harmony and show the power of a Living God in enabling the two of you to blend these differences together? I've asked a number of people, "Would you enjoy being married to someone identical to you and if so, what would that be like?" So far no one has replied in the affirmative. Remember that you and your partner were created by God as irreplaceable individuals, far different from any others on this earth. God considers you to be a talented and unique person of indescribable worth to Him. Enjoy your value and your spouse's.

Life-Changers

Identify how much you need your partner's characteristics.

Allow God to bring forth your undeveloped area.

". . . be of the same (agreeable) mind one with another; live in peace . . ."

Honor Christ by submitting to each other (Ephesians 5:21 TLB).

9

Give Me Power

Power! Control! More power! More control! Nations want power, corporations strive for power, politicians want power, interest groups want power. It seems that everyone has this determined drive to gain more power and control. Marriages are not immune from this unquenchable thirst. In fact, power struggles are one of the biggest perpetrators of conflict in marriages. We hear about specific issues that couples argue about but underlying many of them is a power struggle.

One of the contributing factors in a power struggle is the myth we learned early in life: "If my way is right and valid, then your way must be wrong." This type of thinking does not allow for differences or the ability to learn from others.

Let's listen in on a couple who are quite skilled in their struggle for power. Jim and Nancy have a number of power struggles but a recurring one is his clothing. Nancy is very uncomfortable with Jim's choice of wardrobe. She actually feels embarrassed by the cheap, out-of-style clothes which he continues to wear year after year. Money is not the problem since they make a very comfortable living. Often Nancy will buy him some sharp, up-to-date items, but in a short time he reverts back to his old clothes. She has confronted him about his dressing habits and usually says something like, "You know how much I hate that ridiculous shirt. Do you have to insist on wearing it? It's out of style, doesn't fit, and it's not even your color. Could you please wear the new one I gave you for your birthday?"

Nancy really wants Jim to look better and inwardly he knows that what she is saying is right. But what does he say to her? "You're always telling me what to do. I can dress myself. Why do you have this terrible desire to control me? You even want me to change my hair style each year. I like my clothes. They're me! You're making me look like a wimp!"

Jim realizes he's being stubborn. Nancy also realizes that the harder she tries to get Jim to change, the more he resists. And there are times when he would like to wear the new clothes, but he doesn't want her winning. This is a classic power struggle. But remember this principle: *The more you struggle for power, the less you have!*

Why does Nancy have such a need to control? Why is Jim fearful of being controlled? What are their needs? You see, underneath the need to control and the fear of being controlled are often some issues from our past. When these are faced, confronted and the power stripped from them, we become open to growth and maturity.

Nancy's parental home was chaotic and out of control. Her brothers kept getting into trouble and her parents couldn't keep order. Jim's background included a macho father who said no woman would control him. And when his mother dressed him in nice clothes on Sunday for church, Jim was ridiculed and put down. Could it be that when Nancy tries to change his style of dress, he hears his father's voice?

We have raised Shelties in our home. A Sheltie looks like a miniature collie and is a very intelligent dog—until it gets into a tug-of-war with another puppy. They both sit there and pull and pull on the towel and neither of them gets anywhere. They wear themselves out pulling, trying to get the towel away from the other puppy. If they were really smart they might figure out that what they're doing isn't working. In fact, if one would let up on his end of the towel, it would probably knock the other puppy off balance, dislodge the towel and then the smart puppy could run away with it all to himself.

Sometimes my wife and I sit there and laugh at their antics. Perhaps in reality we are laughing at ourselves for we are not very different from the puppies. Married couples often pull, pull, pull, but nothing is resolved. Neither one is willing to risk a new approach.

During the '60s and '70s, we would read in the newspaper stories of a Japanese soldier on some remote Pacific island, still engaged in fighting World War II. When he gave up or was captured, he was surprised to discover that Japan had lost the war but had grown into a strong and prosperous nation once again. And now he could return home and enjoy Japan's new life. By surrendering, he was freed from bondage and fighting and being hunted as a fugitive. Surrendering brought freedom and a better life. We tend to engage in wars that don't need to be fought.

As you search through dictionaries, you will discover many definitions for the word "power." One is "the possession of control, authority, or influence over others." The Oxford English Dictionary defines authority as "power or right to enforce obedience . . . the right to command or give an ultimate decision." Therefore, in a marital relationship when one partner has the bulk of the power or authority, he or she has most of the control and makes most of the decisions! The person on the other side ends up feeling inferior, dependent, abused, neglected and downtrodden with attitudes of dejection, anger and resentment.

Did you know that in most conflicted marriages, the partners are *unaware* of how much power each one has and emotionally feels the partner has far more power than he or she deserves?[1] When we speak of power in a marriage relationship, we are talking about the ability of one spouse to influence or change the behavior of the other. The one with the greatest power is usually the one who somehow controls the actions of the other person. But how? Perhaps through making most of the decisions or through having control over the finances or making more money. There may be an exception to this concept, however. When you look at a marriage in which one earns and controls the money, initially it may seem that the breadwinner has more power. But this may be offset by the wife who stays home, is very satisfied with her role and has great influence in the areas of child-rearing, social life, directing where the finances are spent—or by having a greater knowledge about running the home than her spouse.

Unfortunately, there are some spouses who are trapped and kept in a posture of dependency by a partner who deals out the finances when he sees fit. This type of helplessness breeds depression, resentment and often major conflicts.

Power struggles can easily emerge when both husband and wife have their own careers. A common question being raised today, compared to a glaring silence on the subject twenty-five years ago, is, "Whose career takes precedence? Which is more important?" In previous decades there was no question. Today economic power and status competition struggles are quite common. Each spouse tends to feel that his or her career is more important and has more impact than the partner's. Today, career women would like to have the same power and equality that is theirs at work extend to their homes. Many traditions have fallen away during the past fifteen years, and sometimes the debris gets in the way. Numerous marital conflicts arise because of the desire for power to be divided equally between men and women. The conflict emerges because the marriage becomes an area of competition rather than a unified pulling together.

Marriage is a miniature example of the body of Christ where each one contributes because of his or her own unique ability. Competition may be less when the husband is the primary breadwinner and the wife has a supportive role within the home. Or there could be less competition if a wife sees her working as a job rather than a career. Then the family's life is still seen as dependent upon what the husband accomplishes.

Competition can become a major issue when a wife advances faster than her husband and eventually moves ahead of him. Anger, resentment and distancing often occur, yet they do not have to exist. But not too many couples would admit to being in competition with one another. This competition may arise from the core of feelings of insecurity and threats to one's identity. But these are unnecessary threats if the source of our identity and security in Jesus Christ is realized! Which marriages survive when the woman earns more or achieves more than her husband? Marriages in which both individuals have a strong sense of self-esteem, respect for one another, and a willingness to support and encourage one another.

An overlooked arena for marital authority struggles is emotional power. This can be even more serious than the other problems mentioned. When a person is told what to do most of the time, when decisions are made for that person, when he or she looks to the other person as the authority, we have emotional dependency. There are some couples who are comfortable with this style. Many others are quite frustrated. A wife told me, "I wish I had some say in what we do or where we go. But my husband always overrides me and I end up thinking that he is right. His ideas do make sense and he is able to decide so quickly. It takes me longer and I tend to waver back and forth with my decisions. But sometimes I just wish I could have some say . . . ."

Not everyone who holds the power is content with that style of relationship. A husband reflected, "I wish she wasn't so dependent on me. I would like her to make some decisions, stick with them and carry them out. There are times I get so frustrated with having to make decisions which are so simple and ridiculous. Why can't she make up her mind? I even get phone calls at work about simple decisions. I feel like a parent!"

In a healthy marriage relationship, each person leans on the other from time to time. But because of our culture, dependency has become a problem word. We are taught to be independent and self-sufficient. We put little value on being dependent, so who wants to admit they *are* dependent? We all struggle with problems in our lives that we can't solve by ourselves. We need the help of another person. There are some emotional needs that cannot be satisfied alone. A marital relationship can provide the most intense and enduring support.

There are times in a marriage when each spouse parents the other by giving assistance and comfort. That's all right if the roles switch back and forth and each person maintains his or her own identity.

A husband shared with me, "At work, I'm seen as being strong and sometimes even tough by the others. But if they only knew. There are days when I doubt my abilities, my decisions, even if I'm in the right job. I can't share that stuff with them. But I can share it with my wife. She's safe and she knows how to listen. Sometimes she reassures me and gives me advice, but mostly she just accepts me. Yeah, I guess I depend upon her at those times and that's all right. I like it and I need it. Other times she sure depends on me." A healthy marriage is one in which the partners take turns leaning upon one another.[2]

There are many times when I'm dependent upon Joyce for emotional support, suggestions, insights, comfort, encouragement and decisions. There are decisions I would prefer she make. At other times, she is dependent upon me. After almost thirty years of marriage we are still refining this process.

When couples have disagreements, often they are not fighting over the problem they think they are. Frequently the disagreement is over who's going to be in control of the relationship at that moment. Many couples compete for both power and attention. Underlying the need for attention is the desire to feel recognized or significant.

Have you ever heard a person correcting his or her spouse in public? Let me give you some examples. Perhaps you've heard these or even been embroiled in this type of discussion yourself.

Joe and Sadi were talking with friends of theirs and were asked how large their new home was. Sadi said, "It's 2500 square feet." John said, "Oh, no dear. It's not that much." Sadi looked startled and said, "Why, it is 2500 square feet." John replied with "No, *dear,* it isn't. It's 2470 square feet."

Later as they talked with another couple John was overheard to say, "Living in our new home will take us longer to get to our offices by another twenty minutes, but it will be worth it." This time Sadi commented with, "Oh, it won't be that much. I think it will add just about fifteen minutes on a normal day." John looked at her with tight lips and said, "I drove it the other day and it took twenty minutes."

Couples argue about how long, how big, how small, what color—all seemingly insignificant facts. But are they really debating over facts? They may think so. I hear this kind of debate all the time in my office. But the real issue is not the facts or who is right or wrong—the issue is who is going to control the relationship. Power! Power! Power!

Some of these arguments are so intense, it's as though each is fighting for survival. If they have an intense need to be in control, it *is* survival and that's why the emotions become so intense.

When both couples have definite ideas and strong wills, defining *"who's in charge in what area"* is the best way to maintain harmony. The difficulties come when clarification or precedent has been set for carrying out tasks. This is true in the home and just as true when couples work together outside the home.

I just returned from running an errand to the store. I know the couple who own the store and the wife was sharing with me how, with the Lord's help, they had turned their marriage around. As she talked about some of the areas of conflict, I made the comment, "It sounds like it could have been a power struggle." Her face lit up and she said, "That's exactly it! It was a real power struggle. Now we're learning to identify our areas of expertise and responsibility."

When you're both used to being in charge, you have to identify the areas. And if one is more dominant than the other, and the spouse is used to being a follower, it is vital to encourage the more submissive one to enter into decisions and become more independent.

You might be thinking, *But won't that encourage a power struggle?* No, power struggles do not have to occur between strong individuals. It's what you do with your strength that makes the difference. A couple I know, the Walters, shared with me how they were making their marriage work. He told me, "The last five years of marriage have been great. We don't see one another as competitors as we did during the first ten years. I married her because of her strength and capabilities, and she married me for the same reason. But at first it was like two stubborn rhinos butting heads for the same territory.

"Now I take charge of what is done outside the home and Jean takes care of the decisions inside the house. We've defined the territory. It doesn't mean that we don't share our viewpoint, but we know who has the final decision and who has more expertise in that area. I plan the vacations, keeping in mind what Jean enjoys, and she takes care of all our social life. That's a relief to me. When we have people over from church, she runs it and I'm the helper. We both know what to do when people come over. We've learned to work together and it sure is easier. Sometimes we have to take the attitude, 'So what if the other person decides or gets their way? Big deal.' We have learned to be more mature and it's helpful." In a marriage there are many occasions when you need one person to be in charge and the other to be a helper. This sounds a little like the scriptural concept of servanthood, doesn't it?

Define your roles in advance and work out some ground rules to follow when unexpected situations arise. For example, you might agree not to correct your partner in public on minor, insignificant items. And it might help to turn to one another and ask, "Was I correct in what I said?" What a difference that would make!

In marriage, many power issues and conflicts are tied into the differences between what "he wants" and "she wants," what "he needs" and "she needs," what "she expects" and "he expects." Other power struggles occur not over the need to control but because of the fear of being controlled. The possession and use of power determines how and when decisions are made in a marriage.

Power is manifested in many ways. Let's consider some of the most common power styles. Perhaps you can identify your own and your spouse's.

One is called the *Passive Submissive.* Outwardly this individual usually follows his spouse's leading and decision-making. Often, he likes his partner to make the decisions and take the load off him—and he prefers being dependent. Perhaps his spouse enjoys this tendency. The balance in the marriage is maintained unless one of them begins to change. And then everything begins to fall apart. On a scale of 0–10, indicate with a check mark where you would fall on this power style. Put an X to indicate where you feel your partner falls.

0	5	10
NOT AT ALL	*JUST AVERAGE*	*DEFINITELY*

The *Passive Aggressive* appears to be a follower but has great ability to sabotage the decisions. This person does not manifest any outward show of power but is highly proficient at manipulation. "Outwardly compliant but inwardly a rebel" is the name of the game. This person tends to be late, forgetful, makes vague put-down statements which leave his or her partner wondering what was said. He/she goes along with a decision but then does something to make it lose its value. This person might agree to take a short vacation camping but acts inept, negative or burns every meal. The trip isn't worth the hassle!

Why are people like this? Many have never learned to come straight out with their desires. They are afraid of confrontation, rejection and being disappointed. And they deny how much power they have! On a scale of 0–10, indicate with a check mark where you would fall on this power style. Put an X to indicate where you feel your partner falls.

0	5	10
NOT AT ALL	*JUST AVERAGE*	*DEFINITELY*

Have you ever heard of the *Passive Sufferer?* This is another way that power is displayed. He/she goes along with the partner's decisions, but suffers as a result. His/her suffering may be used to get back at the partner, to bring about guilt or to display self-righteousness. Often this person lets others know in his/her own way how much he/she is suffering. Such people have gone to the college of martyrdom for their degree. On a scale of 0–10, indicate with a check mark where you would fall on this power ladder. Use an X to indicate where you feel your partner falls.

0	5	10
NOT AT ALL	*JUST AVERAGE*	*DEFINITELY*

The *Assertive-Controlling* person tends to insist that his/her demands be met. This person feels that he or she has won when the partner gives in. And the point of winning is what's important—more so than the issue. This comes at the partner's expense, however. On a scale of 0–10, indicate with a check mark where you would fall on this power style. Put an X to indicate where you feel your partner falls.

0	5	10
NOT AT ALL	*JUST AVERAGE*	*DEFINITELY*

The ideal response is the *Assertive-Adapter.* This person can openly assert his needs to his spouse but is also willing to adapt to meet his partner's demands. This unique person is comfortable using power *and* relinquishing power—a rare combination. In the relationship where both parties are assertive adapters, each knows the beliefs and values of his or her partner. He also knows his own needs will be taken into consideration. Opinions of others are considered. On a scale of 0–10, indicate with a check mark, where you would fall on this power style. Put an X to indicate where you feel your partner falls.

0 X O	5	10
NOT AT ALL	*JUST AVERAGE*	*DEFINITELY*

Now go back over the categories and this time consider which issues of decision-making in your marriage fall under the various categories. It is not uncommon for a partner to respond one way in a particular issue and then shift to another pattern of power display for another issue. It sounds strange but it does happen from time to time. Just write in the decision issue if you can identify any.[3]

To help you identify the balance and display of power in your marriage let's consider how decisions are made in a number of common areas of marriage. This should help you identify what is occurring in your own relationship. First read statements "a" through "e" below.

a. I like my spouse to take the lead and make decisions in this area.
b. I let my spouse make decisions in this area, but often resent it and subtly resist it.
c. My spouse makes decisions in this area. I go along but oftentimes suffer and feel that I'm sacrificing.
d. I am pretty good at asserting my needs in this area, but I can compromise.
e. I assert my needs in this area, but have a difficult time when compromise is required.

Below is a list of decisions that commonly get made in marriages. Next to each decision, place the letter corresponding to the statement above that is most suited to how you feel about the way the decision gets made in your marriage:

____ choosing what leisure activity to do together.
____ deciding how often we clean our home.
____ making major purchases for our home, like furniture, a dishwasher, etc.
____ making major purchases for outside our home, like a car, a lawn mower, etc.
____ deciding who initiates sex.
____ deciding how often to see family.
____ deciding how much money we save.
____ deciding how often to entertain friends and family.
____ deciding where to live.
____ deciding how to celebrate special occasions, like birthdays and holidays.
____ choosing cards and gifts for family members.
____ deciding how committed we are to our jobs.
____ other (Please identify).[4]

Once you've completed the above list, examine it carefully to identify those areas in which you and your spouse do and do not have problems relating to power. If you feel satisfied with the way the decision is handled in your marriage, place a check next to it on the list. Circle each decision not being handled to your satisfaction.

As you may have guessed, the letters next to the statements above correspond to the five categories we listed earlier. The letter "a" corresponds to being "Passive-Submissive," the letter "b" to "Passive-Aggressive," the letter "c" to "Passive-Suffering," the letter "d" to "Assertive-Adapter," and the letter "e" to "Assertive-Controlling."

It would be impossible for me to determine which of the issues listed above are problematic for you based on which letter you placed next to them. Only *you,* as a couple, can decide when the balance of power in your relationship is a problem for your marriage.

Now that you've had the opportunity to identify these issues, let's move toward making some changes if they are needed. Let's identify where you would like to change:

1. Please list the areas of decision making that you would like to be more involved in and indicate the extent.

2. What areas of decision-making does your partner want to be more involved in and to what extent? Can you think of why he or she would like to be more involved?

3. Please identify the areas of decision-making your spouse would like you more involved in and the areas you would like him or her more involved in.

4. If you were to ask your partner the question, "Are there areas of decision-making you would like me less involved in?" what would he or she say?

5. Are there areas of decision-making you would like your partner less involved in? If so, what are they and what is your reason?[5]

Be sure you take the time to discuss your responses. Share with your partner first of all what you have learned about yourself by doing this.

The Murrays were having problems and had made an appointment with their medical doctor simply because there were no marriage counselors in their town. They didn't know who else to turn to and they were tired of the pain and conflict which existed in their marriage. They sat down with their doctor and Jean began to talk:

Jean: I've had it with this TV addict I'm married to. He comes home, says a few words to me and the kids and then heads for the tube. I swear, I think he's addicted to it. And the weekends are the worst. Anything that smells like sports, he's lost.

Frank: Well, it's the only relaxation I ever get. And if I even look up for a minute you're right there with that darned list of projects you've been saving up forever. I need to unwind.

Jean: I don't mind unwinding, but there's a limit. You're so unwound . . .

Frank interrupted: Stow it, will you! I've heard it all before, Doctor. This goes on and on and I'd like some relief from her griping.

At this point their doctor asked a couple of questions:

Doctor: Jean, when he retreats to the TV, what do you do?

Jean: I usually get angry, try to interrupt him and get his attention and find out when he can help or even talk to us. I bang around in the room and probably try to disturb his TV time as much as possible.

Doctor: But you really want his attention and involvement?

Jean: Yes.

Doctor: Frank, what do you do when she gets after you?

Frank: I just watch more TV and tune her out to try to get away from her.

Doctor: But you really want her to back off and give you some peace and quiet. Right?

Frank: That's correct.

Doctor: Well, it seems to me that each of you has really perfected a style of trying to get each other to do what you want and it's one big giant failure, isn't it? How does it feel to live with being a failure all these years?

Naturally they were both a bit shocked to hear such a straightforward approach. But it was true. The doctor took out his prescription pad and wrote on it for a few minutes, then he said, "Here's a prescription that I've written out for you. It has the diagnosis of your problem, the prognosis or what you can expect to happen and the treatment and prescription. I want you to take this home, open it up there and read it and come back to see me next week with your own suggested treatment plan in writing. If either of you fails to bring it in writing, I'll just send you home since you'll be wasting your time and mine. I like results. I like my patients to get well. I'll see you next week."

The Murrays took the folded prescription and when they arrived home they opened and read it. Here is what it said:

Diagnosis—Vicious circle.

Prognosis—If it's not cut out, it's like a cancer. It destroys. If it's removed and replaced with new positive responses, the marriage will grow.

Treatment and Prescription—Giving up old habit patterns and ways of responding and creating new ways of viewing and responding to your partner.

What's a vicious circle? There are three characteristics. One is, the harder each person tries to deal with an issue or problem, the worse it gets. The second is, each partner is looking more to his or her own intentions rather than on the consequences of what he or she is doing. Finally, each person is convinced that the way out of this is just to try harder in order to make his or her partner change.

A simple way to describe it is: The more you try the worse it gets. You try to get your partner to open up and talk and he becomes quieter. You try to get more time with your partner and instead, she avoids you more. Why? Because what each of you is doing sets the other person off. Both partners become more stubborn and set in their way of doing whatever they are doing. Each person is actually afraid of changing because of his or her fear that things will get worse than they are at the present time. How do you change? Simple, just refuse to play your part in the game. Do something different.

Do you have any vicious circles operating in your marriage? What are they? What part do you play in the circle and what part does your partner play? Is there a power struggle involved in this process?

Remember the thought expressed earlier in this book? *If what you've been doing isn't working, there has to be a better way.* To help you break loose from a vicious circle and many of the power struggles in your marriage, complete the following in writing:

1. Identify a problem between you and your partner that you feel is a vicious circle.

2. Write out in detail what it is that your partner does or doesn't do that is making the problem worse.

3. Now, write out in detail what you do either as a direct response to what your partner does or as your effort to change it.

4. What have you hoped that your partner's response would be or what have you felt that it should be?

5. What has been his or her actual response up to now?

6. Describe how you feel about this response.

7. Have you shared this feeling with your partner in such a way that your spouse understands? How did he or she respond to you?

8. Describe your fear of doing something different from what you're doing now. What could be worse than what's happening now?

9. List what you would be willing to try that would be different. Don't be concerned with what your partner should do differently.

10. The next step is to select what you will do differently, write out in detail what you will say and do, and practice in your mind and out loud. Then commit your new response in prayer to the Lord and ask for His guidance to both remember and do this the next time. When *you* do something different it will break the pattern. And you will feel much better knowing that you are no longer contributing to the problem.[6]

Robert A. Schuller talked about his parents and what has worked for them in *The Positive Family:*

> My mother, Arvella Schuller, shares her secret for how she and my father could be married successfully for over thirty years, even though they don't always agree. She explains that they have a scale of nonapproval. When she and Dad disagree, they measure the depth of the intensity of nonagreement on a scale of one to ten:

1. The lowest level is, "I'm not enthusiastic, but go ahead if you want to." From there the intensity of the comments increases.

2. "I don't see it the way you do, but I may be wrong, so go ahead."

3. "I don't agree. I'm sure you're wrong. But I can live with it. Go ahead."

4. "I don't agree, but I'll be quiet and let you have your way. I can change it to my way later on. Next year I can repaint, repaper, reupholster it my way."

5. "I don't agree, and I cannot remain silent. I love you, but I will not be able to keep from expressing my disapproval. So don't be offended if you hear me expressing a contrary view."

6. "I do not approve, and I make a motion we postpone and delay action until we both are able emotionally and rationally to re-evaluate our positions. Give me more time."

7. "I strongly disapprove. This is a mistake—costly, not easily corrected—and I stand firm. I cannot and will not go along with it."

8. "My answer is no! I will be so seriously upset if you go ahead that I cannot predict what my reaction will be."

9. "No way! If you go ahead I have to tell you I quit; I'll walk out!"

10. "No—no—no! Over my dead body!"

My father maintains that in more than thirty years of marriage he and Mom never went above a six in their level of disagreement. As I think back to growing up in their home, I would say that he is correct, for the most part. They may have hit a seven or an eight once or twice, but they usually stopped at number six, which really means, "I love you very, very much. Since I can't tell you what this is going to do to our relationship, which is obviously more important than the decision, let's wait and think about it . . . give me time to see your viewpoint and feel what you feel."[7]

How can you disengage from your power struggles? Be a risk taker. So what if it doesn't work the first time? You did something positive just by doing something new. If you want to go back to the power struggle, go ahead. But you probably won't want to. It's not that you're giving up your old style or response all at once. You still have the option of returning. You've just rented out the old house, you didn't burn it down. Here's another approach you might take:

1. Make a list of as many things that your partner should do and would do if he or she really cared about you, but doesn't do at this time.

2. Now choose two or three items that are a real pain for you at the present time. Place each one at the top of a page, then begin writing some new options that you could select to replace your old pattern.

Let's consider an example of something that is quite common. Mary is a very organized person and likes to take on her responsibilities in an orderly fashion. Her husband has the task of paying the monthly bills. But he's constantly late and often will forget them for an entire month unless Mary reminds and nags him. It seems the more she does this the more he procrastinates. Each month they go round and round over the same issue. What are the options?

a. Give up all control and influence. She could tell him that from this point on she will let him take full charge of paying the bills. Since he said he wants to be in charge of that, he can be. She will not say another word about it if bill collectors call or the utilities get shut off. He will have to take the responsibility of dealing with the problem.

b. A second option is to just do it herself. It may take less energy than pressuring her husband.

c. A third option is to ask him how she could assist him with paying the bills each month. Does he want reminders? Does he want any help? Is writing the checks a pain to him? Would he prefer they do it together? Would it help to do it over a nice dinner at home or elsewhere? Would he like to make a party out of it? Give him a number of sane and crazy options. In other words, do something different and unexpected.[8]

Do you have a vicious circle working with your partner? Take a close look. Without even knowing it, you both may be working together to intensify a problem you'd really like to cut out of your life. Why cooperate over something you don't want?

Do you want to know how to break the pattern of a power struggle? There are two steps involved. Open up your perspective enough to see your spouse's viewpoint. Then allow his or her perspective to help you loosen your hold on your own viewpoint. When you do this, your partner may stop fighting you. This doesn't mean you allow the other partner to dominate and walk all over you. It means you are flexible enough to see both sides and allows you to see different perspectives and new options. The choice is yours.

Life-Changers

Identify who has power and how it's used.

Learn to be an assertive adapter.

Giving up your power struggle gives you freedom.

. . . let every man be quick to hear, (a ready listener) slow to speak . . . (James 1:19 AMP)

10

It's Not What You Say . . . or Is It?

Join me as we listen in to a conversation between Kurt and Heather. What you are going to hear is fairly typical of their conversations. How would you evaluate their interaction? What suggestions would you give them as they try to resolve a conflict?

Heather: Do you think there is any way we can work out a schedule or a plan—a basic plan—for when things will get done?

Kurt: Sure, if we work on it together. But you know how to do as many things as I know how to do.

Heather: No, I don't!

Kurt: Yes, you do! You're just being stubborn. And it's safe for you to say that you don't because then there is no pressure on you to do it. But *you do know* how to do it. It just feels like you don't know how to do it! A lot of things that I am doing, I am doing for the first time myself. So I have just as much experience or inexperience as you do, and a lot of that stuff is not necessarily important for you to wait for me to do it—*if* it is so important that it get done right away!

Heather: Well, I can paint in the bedroom. I can do that painting you asked me to do, but what I plan for the kitchen . . . is not something that I could have done if we were going to paint what's there now. But *if* you are going to rebuild the kitchen, *I can't do that.* I *don't want* to do that. What are you thinking that I can . . . ?

Kurt (interrupting): Is it that you can't do it or you don't want to do it—or both?

Heather: Both, I don't want to do the kitchen! I will paint, I will finish the kitchen and I'll do all the painting. But if that is not what you want, then I feel like you need to take charge of that.

Kurt: Well, there are other projects though.

Heather: Like? (She's really defensive now.)

Kurt: The den.

Heather: What about the den?

Kurt: The organization of things in the den and I mean full organization.

Heather: I feel like we need our Friday nights that we scheduled and they haven't happened. I need you there. (She's intense.)

Kurt: Why?

Heather: Because everything is on the bed right now. I can't label those files. I put everything in stacks in files. I can't label them. I don't know what they are. I need you there to answer questions. I can do part of it, but I can't do all of it.

Kurt: How about the fireplace?

Heather: Fireplace. Sanding the fireplace?

Kurt: Yes.

Heather: Doesn't that have to be done with a machine?

Kurt: No.

Heather: I guess I feel stubborn on some of those things because those are things that you want done and *I don't want to do them.*

Kurt: You don't want them done?

Heather: I don't like doing it myself.

Kurt: Neither do I.

Heather: (Emphatically) Well, I will do what I can. Period!

(It seems Kurt and Heather are at a stand-off. A power struggle has emerged. What could Kurt and Heather do at this time? What would you suggest?)

Kurt: I don't want you to have to feel that you have to do any of it on your own. But I would like us to be able to talk about it. In other words, I am not expecting you to do everything that is not done. But I would like to talk about it with the consideration that you are capable and able to do more. Just by virtue of the fact that you're a woman and you have never done things, doesn't mean that you can't learn or make mistakes like I do in the process of doing things. I'll be happy with whatever you do. I will be happy with it *just* because you do it. You put effort into doing something different since that's more important to me than how the finished product turns out.

Heather: I guess I feel like we would want different things. I think we just need time working together on things like that. That would help me to do what I need to do.

Kurt: OK. How?

Heather: Just talking through things, putting it on paper. Paper is important to me. That would be a real help if we could get it on paper. I respond best to what I see.

Kurt: Get what on paper?

Heather: A plan for repairs. A plan for anything. I would settle for anything.

Kurt: What do you mean anything? You're always so general. Get specific.

Heather: Goals, goals of any kind. Either for repairs in the house or for something else. Remember, the chapter in the book that we read about setting short term and long term goals. That would accomplish a lot.

Kurt and Heather communicate as though life is a contest. Marriage was not designed to be competitive, we make it that way.

Since you weren't there to actually hear the conversation, you wouldn't know that at times the tone of their voices was quite intense and their body posture resistant. How would you evaluate their conversation? Well, before you decide, read on. Then, using the principles presented on what to do and what to avoid, go back and analyze their conversation.

I'm going to make some radical statements regarding your communication. This chapter may not be exactly what you expected. But I hope it will accomplish two goals: First, to give you some new direction and tools so your communication will dampen the fires of conflict instead of fanning the flames. Second, to direct you to resources that will help you build a new, creative, positive communication style. The guidelines presented here are designed to settle conflicts.

Let me share with you some key principles that can help you bring about the changes you are seeking. Here they are.

The Word of God

Your communication will change when you begin to put into practice the principles from the finest Book *ever* written on communication—the Word of God! Are you aware that the Bible gives us the guidelines we need for healthy communication? Start reading the Book of Proverbs and as you read, underline every passage that refers to communication. You will be amazed at what you will discover. I suggest you use the Living Bible version. Choose a passage each day to begin memorizing and personalizing. Visualize yourself using this passage in your communication with others. The scripture is not just a better way. It's the *best* way!

Let's consider some of the passages from the Book of Proverbs. These illustrate the effects of negative talk as well as the benefits of positive communication. Please look these up in the Living Bible and write or type them out on a piece of paper and read them every morning and evening for one month:

Proverbs 10:19	Proverbs 11:12	Proverbs 11:18
Proverbs 12:16	Proverbs 12:18	Proverbs 12:22
Proverbs 12:25	Proverbs 13:3	Proverbs 15:1
Proverbs 15:4	Proverbs 15:23	Proverbs 16:24
Proverbs 17:9	Proverbs 17:27–28	Proverbs 18:13
Proverbs 19:11	Proverbs 20:3	Proverbs 25:11–12
Proverbs 26:28	Proverbs 28:13	Proverbs 29:11
Proverbs 29:20		

Speak Your Partner's Language

Your communication will change when you learn to speak your partner's language! When you married, you chose a foreigner. That's right. You chose a person who may be the same nationality and race as you, but he or she still came from a culture with different values, beliefs, customs and even a different language. One of you may be an amplifier and the other a condenser. One is more visual and the other is more auditory. One goes for the bottom line and the other verbally rambles around the meadow. One of you keeps time via a stopwatch and the other uses a calendar. You use the same words but they have different meanings. One of you may be direct and straightforward and the other cautious and tentative. Enough said?

I have a bias. I believe the reason so many couples feel misunderstood, unloved and in continual conflict is that they have never learned to speak the same language. Not only do we need to learn to speak the same language to resolve conflicts, we also need to speak the same love language in order for the romantic side of our marriage to bloom.

How will you learn to speak your partner's language? Is it really possible? Yes, it is. (Since this has been discussed extensively before, let me refer you to my book, *How to Speak Your Spouse's Language,* published by Fleming H. Revell.) When you are attempting to resolve differences and problem-solve, you have to use your partner's language and way of thinking. It can be done.

Your communication will change when you understand the unique way in which men and women differ in their communication patterns and the way in which they think. There are definite differences between the sexes, which were shared in an earlier chapter. Many of these are culturally developed and reinforced. Others are caused by the way in which God created us. Understanding and accepting these, and using this knowledge to help you speak your partner's language, will help diminish the conflicts and hassles in a marriage (or any relationship, for that matter).

Rules

Your communication will change as you create a new set of communication rules or guidelines to follow when you communicate. Everyone communicates via a set of rules. Unfortunately, most people never sit down and create these rules; they usually just evolve. Many of these rules are negative and self-defeating. Let's rephrase my statement from an earlier chapter to apply to communication. If the way you're communicating now isn't working, why keep doing it? There has to be a better way! There is! Let's discover it together.

1. Many marriages are battlefields littered with the remains of men and women who never came to the peace table to negotiate a settlement. There are some principles you can follow which will keep a minor altercation from becoming World War III. Many of the conflicts that couples experience begin with an accusation. This could be in the form of a gripe, criticism or complaint. The person receiving the complaint usually feels it's invalid. What typically happens then is that the spouse proceeds to explain why it wasn't valid or retaliates in some manner. What does this do to the person who initially shared the complaint or criticism? Further retaliations occur, of course, and the war escalates. When the accuser intensifies his or her responses, the conflict is in full stride.

Some people, however, try to handle problems by avoiding bringing up concerns in any way. This allows their spouse to have full rein. They can do whatever they want to do and there's no sharing of concern. This is unhealthy for a number of obvious reasons:

a. When a spouse is truly frustrated and has no outlet, there is a tendency to build resentment. Unfortunately, in time resentment breeds indifference or could lead to volcanic eruptions or even physical illness.

b. Distrust begins to cripple your spouse's ability to hear your feelings and thus intimacy in the relationship is crippled.

c. Even if an accusation is shared in an appropriate manner, there is still valid information there which could provide growth for the relationship. But it is neither heard nor received.

Let me share with you a myth that goes like this: "It's better to talk than to listen because you will have more influence and control in a relationship." That is not true. The listener controls the *conversation* but not the speaker. Most of us operate under the myth that the more we talk, the more we influence the listener. If both people in a conversation believe this, the talking escalates and becomes more intense, which is quite sad, because the words fly through the air with nowhere to land. Deafness prevails!

What do I mean by the statement that the listener controls the conversation? Compare the listener to the driver of a car. The one talking is like the engine. The engine provides the power, but the person at the wheel has the power to decide where the car will go. You, the listener, can give direction and guide the flow of the conversation by the statements you make and the questions you ask.

Statements such as the following can guide and lead:

"That's an interesting thought. Can you tell me a bit more how that will . . . ?"

"Does that mean . . . ?"

"If I understand what you are saying . . . ."

This last statement is what is called paraphrasing. It reinforces the person talking so that he or she will continue to talk. When you verbally agree with the talker, you cause the person to share even more.

One other thought about the listener. Some people say, "When I listen, it seems to cause the other person to just talk and talk and talk. Why?" Perhaps initially it does, but if you remain perfectly silent, you create such tension within the person speaking that he begins to back off. By not responding, you let the other individual know that you have completed your part of the conversation. However, I am not advocating use of the silent treatment, that devastatingly unfair weapon which in time will erode a relationship.

Why do we need to listen to other people? There are four basic reasons to listen to other people:

a. To understand the other person.
b. To enjoy the other person.
c. To learn something from the one talking (such as learning his or her language!).
d. To give help, assistance or comfort to the person.

The world is made up of many pseudo-listeners who masquerade as the real product. But anyone who has not listened for the above reasons does not really listen. Proverbs 20:12

says, "The hearing ear and the seeing eye, the Lord has made both of them."

Often when we listen, we have mixed motives. But when we listen without a filter or preconceived opinions we will be able to really hear what our partner is *attempting* to say. James 1:19 calls us to "be a ready listener." Be sure to listen to your partner with your eyes since over 55 percent of what he or she says is nonverbal. (For additional help on listening and nonverbal communication be sure to read *How to Speak Your Spouse's Language* mentioned elsewhere in this chapter.)

2. Watch out for all-night discussions, especially if one of you tends to be a brief communicator. Too much talk is an overload for that partner. Talking for several hours or well into the morning is usually counterproductive. In the field of counseling we have learned that having shorter periods of time (45 minutes to 1 hour) with a starting and stopping time is more effective than three-hour sessions. The longer you talk in a conflictual situation, the more exhausted you will feel because your adrenalin is running longer. Usually the person who keeps the discussion alive is planning that the longer he or she talks, the more hope there is for change. However, marathon discussions usually block effective communication and the runners drop out exhausted. Look back at the list of passages from Proverbs. Do these passages say anything about this rule?

3. Don't be a grudge collector. No, I didn't say a garbage collector. I said a grudge collector. Grudge-collecting is keeping a mental list of all the ways your partner has hurt you. And often you remember what it was and your spouse doesn't. I hope I don't get into too much difficulty with this next statement, but women do tend to remember grievances and hurts longer than men do. This is due to their ability to focus on details and their interpersonal sensitivity. Men usually release issues quickly. Grudges are endless, and they don't necessarily have the same level of importance either. Broken promises, appointments, forgotten anniversaries, being late, criticisms—all are remembered more than the delightful times, the compliments, romantic occasions, encouraging comments and so on. Grudges fall into the category of a habit. And often the habit exists because of the baggage we brought with us into marriage that should have been discarded earlier in life.

4. When you communicate, be sure to express what you are thinking, feeling or wanting *now* in your relationship with your partner. And put it in your partner's language. Don't dwell on the past. Unfortunately, each time an unpleasant experience happens it sears a response into our emotional receiver. Our minds become conditioned to expect the hurtful but familiar occurrence. Why not try a completely new response on your part?

5. Express whatever you are saying in positive terms. Let your spouse know what you want, not what you don't want—what you are for, not what you're against. Saying, "I want you to listen" is better than, "Why don't you ever listen to me?" I've always wondered what would happen if a partner would honestly share why he or she doesn't listen! The answer might *not* be well received by the questioner! Any concern shared must have specific positive suggestions for improvement as part of the request for change. I've actually heard some people say, "I want you to change and you have to figure it out. I'm not going to tell you what to do." That is a totally unfair statement. A better statement would be: "I would appreciate it if you would . . . ."

If the concern you mention is a behavior or condition that is yours as well, it shouldn't be shared until you have become a positive model for your partner. If you are concerned about your partner's sloppiness or lateness, and *you* also reflect this behavior, use your energy on yourself first. Then perhaps your partner will be more open to hearing your concern.

When you share a concern, ask yourself, "What part do I have in this problem? Am I helping to create this in any way?" Examples: Your husband is often late—"What am I doing to make him late? How do I help him be on time?"

Your wife is often angry—"What do I say or do that triggers her anger?"

Your partner clams up in a discussion—"What might I be doing that makes it difficult for him/her to talk?"

6. When you have feelings to express that you know will be upsetting to your spouse, share mixed feelings at the same time. What do I mean? I recently saw an example of this in counseling. A wife shared with her husband the following statement: "I want to share this with you but I've held back.

I'm sort of reluctant because I don't want to hurt you and upset you. But it's so important to me and our relationship. I feel so alone and isolated when . . . ."

7. *What to avoid as you communicate:*

a. *Interrupting*

Keith: "Well, I think that the best alternative would be for you to . . ."

Shirley: "No, I can't go along with . . ."

Keep away from interruptions because they frustrate your partner and show that you're not listening well. Listen to your partner, and wait for him or her to finish. Interruptions may occur both when a partner is actively talking and when he or she has paused for a moment. They should be stopped in both instances. By not interrupting, I mean, do not interrupt verbally, or by opening your mouth, or rolling your eyes, or by looking around to find an escape route. Many verbal interruptions start with the word, "But . . ."; "Not true"; "What?"; "Hold it," etc.

If you do interrupt, you sidetrack the discussion so the problem isn't resolved, your spouse will become indignant and the conflict will go on and on.

b. *Deciding who is at fault*

Shirley: "You shouldn't have yelled at me when I was late."

Keith: "Well, I wouldn't have if you had been on time."

They're trying to decide who's at fault. It makes people angry to be blamed, and it prevents a couple from working together. Don't argue about whose fault things are. Look for ways to handle the situation that will satisfy both of you.

c. *Trying to establish "the truth"*

Shirley: "You did not come home early, it was late!"

Keith: "I was home on time. It was only . . ."

Each has a different view of how it happened, and neither will change the other's memory. Arguing over the truth of specific details won't help a couple solve the problem, and may make both angry. Don't deny the concern. For one reason, the person expressing the concern is often ready for your denial. When you give consideration to what your spouse is saying, you will lessen the intensity of his or her emotions. Be sure to invite your spouse to amplify on what he or she is sharing. Simply request more information, evidence and positive suggestions for change. This can eliminate a tug of war. You might respond with, "Well, I hadn't really realized I was doing that. I'd like to think about what you've said and I appreciate you bringing it to my attention."

Is that your usual response? How would your partner respond to that? When you definitely feel that the concern is not accurate or nowhere near as frequent as your partner says, you don't have to just agree with it or accept it. But neither do you have to immediately deny it. You could say, "I guess there could be a possibility of that. Let me think about that and let's talk further in an hour." This gives you time to consider what has been shared and to formulate what you would like to say.

d. *Getting sidetracked*

Keith: "Like I said, you leave clothes on the floor."
Shirley: "Well, your desk is always pretty messy, too, you know."

Keith and Shirley are getting off the subject. Remember to stay on one issue at a time. Other issues may seem related, but they get you off the track. Don't respond to a statement or question designated to lead you astray.

e. *Dealing with multifaceted problems*

Keith: "Well, you leave the tub full of water, clothes on the floor, the beds unmade, dishes in the sink."

Whoa! There are many parts to this problem. It is often confusing to deal with many aspects of a large problem at one time. It is best to choose one to work on at a time and try not to overwhelm your spouse.

f. "*Guilting*" *the other person*

Shirley: "You just don't care about my feelings. You hurt me and don't even care."

Statements like that, whether intended or not, imply that your spouse is rotten, horrible and insensitive. This may make the person feel guilty, become angry and want to say something angry back. Train yourself not to use guilt-producing statements such as that.

g. *Making power moves and giving ultimatums*

Keith: "You do that, and I'll leave, or I'll . . ."

Keith just gave Shirley an ultimatum. Ultimatums push people into a corner because they either have to lose face by giving in, or act tough and tell you to go ahead. Either way they may become resentful and the problem does not get solved.

h. *Using gunpowder words—"always" and "never"*
Shirley: "You never come home when you say you will."

Please stay away from the words "always" and "never" because a useless argument can arise over the issue of any possible time the situation did or did not occur.

i. *Using trait names*
Keith: "You're just insensitive."

Keith just called Shirley a name, and that may make her angry. When a spouse labels a partner, it implies that he or she cannot change. It's much better to tell your partner the specific behavior you dislike and what you want.

j. *Mind-reading*
Shirley: "You think I spend too much money."

Uh, oh! Shirley just told Keith what he is thinking, as if she could read his mind. Trying to read the other person's mind isn't good because you could be wrong. Even if you are right, it can make the other person angry to have you speak for him or her. If you want to know what your spouse thinks, ask![1]

k. *Avoid using the weapon of silence*

I call it a weapon because it can be used in defensive and offensive warfare. When silence is used against a partner it feels like rejection and punishment. The silent person is often one who fears rejection. Often he or she has been hurt but does not want to take responsibility for the hurt. Silence isolates couples, widens the gap between them, and will not resolve conflicts. It is a flammable fuel that feeds the fire of conflict.

Over the years of using silence, men and women have learned of its tremendous capabilities. The quiet or silent person usually has the control. Why? Because the person who shares often attempts to get the silent person to talk, using totally ineffective approaches. They plead, talk more, pressure, demand, make threats and become irate, and the more this occurs the deeper the silent partner digs into his or her insulated pit.

Don't fight it. Go with it. Instead of battering the silent

person head on, join him. Consider this approach, "Honey, I realize this is something that is often difficult to talk about. I just want to share my feelings about it. You don't have to say anything. In fact, it would probably be better if you didn't talk about it at this time. Here is what I am concerned about." After it's stated say, "Thank you for listening," and go about your business.

You may be thinking, *That's crazy! That's the very thing that's driving me up the wall! Silence.* That's true. Your spouse's silence is getting to you but now *you* are in charge of his or her silence, not your spouse. You are requesting that your spouse not talk. In a sense, you have just taken control away from the person who was using silence as a power play. How? By encouraging the person to do the very thing that is their power tool. Does this sound strange? Perhaps. But it is highly effective.

If the silence is a power play, the quiet partner often will begin to open up since you're the one making the suggestion. And if talking is basically difficult for the person because he or she never really learned to communicate extensively as a child, the freedom to take one's time, formulate a response, and then share later will be much appreciated. And some people are fearful that a long discussion or disagreement will follow. The assurance that it won't be a long discussion or that a disagreement won't have to be upsetting may open the door to communication.

When you communicate a plan to resolve conflicts, one hopes the communication will not only resolve a problem but will also help to improve the relationship. That's what resolving conflicts is all about—improvement and growth. I've said elsewhere that it is very important to concentrate on the strengths and positive qualities of one another and the relationship. There are also those times when we need to sit down together, identify the problems, what we want to change and then take action. Here is one way to accomplish this:

Each of you take several three-by-five cards. On each card write down a problem which you feel exists in your marriage. In fact, prior to writing this on a card it may help to make a complete list on a separate piece of paper. Arrange your cards in order of importance. Set a time to meet together with a clear starting and stopping point.

Select a card and explain the problem to your spouse, how you feel when it occurs, why it is important to you, and finally suggest what you would like as a solution.

Then your partner shares from a card one of his or her concerns. While each of you is listening, be sure that real listening is taking place. Do not prepare your response or rebuttal while your partner is sharing—and do not interrupt or argue. Accept what is being shared regardless of your hurt or disagreement. Let your partner know that you understand what he or she is sharing perhaps by reflecting or summarizing what you hear. When each of you shares what you would like as a solution, the other should respond with what he or she could do to help.

When you have each completed sharing from your cards, give a summary back to your partner of what you heard the concerns to be. Don't call them gripes or complaints, but concerns. Realize that your spouse's concerns may come from deeper reasons than you are aware of at this time.

The reason for this activity is simple. You have to make the problem clear for each of you to make it part of the solution.[2] After sharing your lists you may discover that many are similar or are tied into one another. It is important for each person to discover the extent of the hurt which each one is experiencing and then clearly indicate what you will do to help solve the problem.

Now that you have some principles and guidelines to follow, let's listen in on a communication exchange which had the potential for a conflict.

We're looking in on Kurt and Heather a few months after their conversation at the beginning of this chapter. One of the other underlying conflicts in their marriage was their yearly vacation. They had been vacationing at the same spot for nine years and Kurt was very comfortable with the choice. For some time, Heather had been wanting to suggest a change, but was hesitant to bring up any suggestions for fear of another argument. She wanted some variety in vacation spots as well as more activity. For the past nine years, they had spent their vacations eating, fishing, loafing and being in the mountains.

One day, Heather became brave enough to try a new approach. She made her suggestion to Kurt:

Heather: Well, Kurt, what do you think about my suggestions?

Kurt: It's new to me. I just don't know . . . . It really comes as sort of a shock. I really like where we've been going and I thought you liked it. We've met a number of new friends there and some come back each year. I don't know about this. I need to think about it.

Heather: That's fine, Kurt. We both need to think more about it. I know you're satisfied there and I have been, too. Why don't we talk about what it is that we've enjoyed so much and what new possibilities may be available in a new vacation spot? We might find some overlap.

Notice that Heather didn't fight Kurt's hesitancy. She acknowledged it and encouraged further discussion. But she also brought the attention back to her suggestion. Another procedure she could have used would be to respond to Kurt's feeling of shock with something like, "I can appreciate your feeling shocked. I can understand why you might feel that way. I guess I'd have similar feelings." Whether you would have the identical feelings or not, you can still validate your spouse's feelings. You are *not* agreeing with facts or ideas.

Heather could also express interest in what Kurt has said by asking, "I'm interested in what you've enjoyed so much about our vacations."

Let's assume that Kurt and Heather continue to discuss and Kurt begins to open up and share additional objections:

Kurt: You know I've really enjoyed kicking back at the lake when we go there. There aren't that many people all over the place and it doesn't take several days to get there. I really look forward to seeing some of those same people each year. They like to fish as much as I do and it's hard to find other fishing addicts like me.

Heather: You really like this place because it's so relaxing for you. It's like a hideaway with a few people you can enjoy.

Kurt: Yeah. I think that's it. I'm not sure a change would have the same enjoyment for me. This place is comfortable, the fishing is always good and I don't know if another place would be as enjoyable.

At this point, Heather could ask Kurt what other information it would take for him to consider making a change. I don't think that Kurt would be expecting this approach and it does indicate that Heather is thoughtfully considering what he likes. She isn't falling into the common trap of telling her spouse only what she wants him to know to convince him of her request.

In a communication exchange such as this it would be easy for one to sidetrack the other. Thus persistence and acknowledgment are important:

Kurt: Why don't we talk about this later? Or better yet, when we do talk about it, let's think it through for the following year and keep on with our plans for the same place in August.

Heather: I can understand that you'd prefer to go to the same place, but I'd like to discuss the possibility of a new location for this year.

Kurt: I don't know. Let's talk about it at another time.

Heather: That's all right with me. But let's set a time to discuss it again for this year.

Kurt: Oh, why don't we just wait and see for awhile . . . .

Heather(after Kurt's pause): I can understand that you'd rather not set a time, but I'd really like to set it now to talk about this year's vacation. And it doesn't mean that we will decide anything during our next discussion. Can we give it a try and set the time?

Naturally the tone of voice and nonverbal expressions will make a world of difference. This conversation is a far cry from the earlier dialogue.

For a number of years I have been sharing a communication covenant with many couples. This covenant was developed by a young couple and they are following the principles. I received their permission to use it and offer this as an example of a positive guide which will work if both partners make the commitment to follow the guidelines. I wouldn't suggest using this as is but as a guide to develop your own. What would guidelines such as these do for your communication?

Communication Covenant

This covenant will be read together each Sunday and then we will ask one another in what way can we improve our application of this covenant in our daily life.

1. We will express irritations and annoyances we have with one another in a loving, specific and positive way rather than holding them in or being negative in general.

a. I will acknowledge that I have a problem rather than stating that you are doing such and such.

b. I will not procrastinate by waiting for the right time to express irritations or annoyances.

c. I will pinpoint to myself the reason for my annoyances. I will ask myself why it is that I feel irritation or annoyance over this problem.

2. We will not exaggerate or attack the other person during the course of a disagreement.

a. I will stick with the specific issue.

b. I will take several seconds to formulate my words so that I can be accurate.

c. I will consider the consequences of what I say before I say it.

d. I will not use the words "always," "all the time," "everyone," "nothing," etc.

3. We will attempt to control the emotional level and intensity of arguments. (No yelling, uncontrollable anger, hurtful remarks.)

a. We will take time-outs for calming down if either of us feels that our own anger is starting to elevate too much. The minimum amount of time for a time-out will be one minute and the maximum ten minutes. The person who feels he needs a greater amount of time to calm down will be the one to set the time limit. During the time-out, each person, by themselves and in writing, will first of all define the problem that is being discussed. Secondly, the areas of agreement in the problem will be listed and then the areas of disagreement will be set out. Also, the three alternate solutions to this problem will be recorded. When we come back together, the person who has been most upset will express to the other individual, "I am interested in what you have written during our time-out and I am willing and desirous of you sharing this with me."

b. Before I say anything, I will decide if I would want this same statement said to me with the same words and tone of voice.

4. We will "never let the sun go down on our anger" or never run away from each other during an argument.

a. I will remind myself that controlling my emotional level will get things resolved quicker and make one less inclined to back off from the problem.

b. I am willing to make a personal sacrifice.

c. I will not take advantage of the other by drawing out the discussion. If we have discussed an issue for 15 minutes, we will then take a time-out and put into practice the written procedure discussed under # 3.

5. We will both try hard not to interrupt the other person when he or she is talking. (As a result of this commitment, there will be no need to keep reminding the other person of his or her responsibility, especially during an argument.)

a. I will consider information that will be lost by interrupting the other person.

b. It is important that the person talking should be concise and to the point.

c. I will remember that the person who was interrupted won't be able to listen as well as if I had waited for my turn.

d. I will put into practice Proverbs 18:13 and James 1:19.

6. We will carefully listen to the other person when he or she is talking (rather than spending that time thinking up a defense).

a. If I find myself formulating my response while the other person is talking I will say, "Please stop and repeat what you said because I was not listening and I want to hear what you were sharing."

b. If we are having difficulty hearing one another, then when a statement is made we will repeat back to the other person what we heard them saying and what we thought they were feeling.

7. We will not toss in past failures of the person in the course of an argument.

a. I will remind myself that a past failure has been discussed and forgiven. True forgiveness means it will not be brought up to the other person again.

b. I will remind myself that bringing up a past failure cripples the other person from growing and developing.

c. If I catch myself bringing up a past failure, I will ask the other person's forgiveness and will then state what it is I am desirous that the other person will do in the future. I will commit myself to this behavior.

8. When something is important enough for one person to discuss, it is equally important for the other person.

a. If I have difficulty wanting to discuss what the other person desires to discuss I will say to them, "I know this topic is important to you and I do want to hear this even though it is a bit difficult for me."

b. In implementing this agreement and all the principles of communication in this covenant we will eliminate outside interferences to our communication such as the radio, television, reading books on our lap, etc. We will look at one another and hold hands during our discussion times.

The principles in this chapter work! They're effective. How do I know? Because so many people have used them as well as myself. This feedback has validated their helpfulness. Many of the principles are not original. They've been gleaned from many sources over the years.

But they won't work for you unless . . .

Do you know what I'm about to suggest? Do you remember what was said in earlier chapters about change? About our habit patterns. How much do you want your communication patterns and conflict level to change?

You'll notice that the last two pages of this chapter are blank. I have nothing to say on them. But you do. Surprised? Now you have the opportunity to do the following:

1. Read back over the suggestions in this chapter.

2. Create your own personal set of rules or communication guidelines that you plan to follow. This may be an activity

that you do as a couple (that would be ideal) or create your own. You can change your own pattern and style of communication regardless of what your partner does. Your change is *not* dependent upon your spouse.

3. Write out in detail your plans and guidelines in the space provided on the last two pages of this chapter.

4. This suggestion may sound crazy, but without it, don't expect much to happen. Read your new plan aloud each morning and evening for the next month. You may feel awkward, embarrassed, self-conscious. That's all right. These feelings will pass and soon this new plan will seep into your mind and become your new style of relating.

5. Commit this plan to God in prayer each day and ask God for the wisdom and direction you need.

6. This suggestion may really get me into hot water. I am interested in the plan you have created. I would enjoy reading your new plan and commitment. If you so desire, make a photocopy of what you have written and mail it to me. I have learned more from other people and their creative ideas than from other books. My address is 1913 E. 17th St., Suite 118, Santa Ana, CA 92701.

Life-Changers

1. Communicate, using the Word of God as your guide.

2. Learn to speak your partner's language.

3. Create your own communication rules or covenant.

Good sense makes a man restrain his anger,
and it is his glory to overlook a transgression
or an offense (Proverbs 11:19 AMP).

11

Anger—a Conflict Crippler!

The discussion had started out quite innocently and calmly. They were sitting at the kitchen table on a Saturday morning having a cup of coffee, looking forward to a leisurely day. No projects, no obligations and no pressure, for a change. They laughed occasionally and talked about their vacation plans for the next month. The atmosphere was light, pleasant and healthy.

An hour later the atmosphere was heavy, unpleasant and bitter. Their voices had climbed to a shrill height. As they glared at each other, their eyes flashed with anger. The words they spoke were spit out and hurled at each other.

What happened? Why the change in this peaceful scene? The discussion concerning their vacation had raised a few differences of opinion and desires. A minor problem that could easily have been worked out had instead ignited a spark of anger in one which quickly spread to the other. There were no firefighters around to douse their anger with fire retardant! The day was ruined, the coffee tasted terrible now and there would be no resolution of the vacation plans on this day.

Anger! A baffling emotion. Although anger is a God-given emotion, most of the time when people become angry the results are negative. Anger is the second major cause of automobile accidents in our country. Anger is involved in the bruised and battered bodies of millions of children and spouses in our nation. Marriages fail because one or both of the marriage partners have never learned to use their anger constructively. Instead, they have allowed their anger to master them instead of learning to master their anger. When anger penetrates a discussion or conflict, it is difficult to come to an acceptable resolution.

If I were to ask you what anger means to you, what would you say? Do you have a definition for it? You feel it, but can you define it? Very simply, anger is a strong feeling of displeasure and irritation. I see a number of people who vent their anger verbally or simply say, "I am so angry!" I wonder what it would be like if they said instead, "I am irritated. I am displeased." This would be far more accurate. But anger soon takes a downhill slide into some other emotional response such as rage, fury or even wrath. Wrath is fervid anger looking for vengeance. Rage is an intense, uncontained, explosive response.

I am concerned about both of the "Big R's"—rage and resentment. When anger erupts into conflicts and goes unresolved, you may begin seeing the two "R's" emerge.

Rage tries to "do in" the other person, to destroy, to take revenge. It uses open warfare. Resentment breeds bitterness and often creates passive-aggressive responses. It's a feeling of indignant displeasure or a persistent ill will against something which you consider a wrong, an insult or an injury. When you resent someone, you create a filter through which you view the person. You become a flaw-finder. Blame is now a major response toward your partner. Often resentment uses guerrilla warfare tactics, hitting and running when your partner is least likely to suspect an attack.

Does this description of rage and resentment tell us anything about its value for resolving conflicts and building harmony in a marriage? As Richard Walters puts it, "Rage blows up the bridges people need to reach each other, and resentment sends people scurrying behind barriers to hide from each other and to hurt each other indirectly."[1] The danger of anger is even indicated by the various ways people try to deal with it. Some pretend they have no anger and bury it. But they bury it alive and in time it tends to destroy them through ulcerated colitis, depression or even a stroke. While it is buried, it is being kept alive by our thoughts.

Some people just let out all their anger and vent it, for they have heard this is healthy. But their misinformation alienates their spouse, their employer and their friends and soon there is no one around to vent their anger upon. Most people feel worse after venting their anger. They feel more irritable, depressed, aggravated, hostile, jittery and unhappy immediately after feeling angry.

Others turn it around on themselves and begin to destroy their self-esteem, their identity and their capabilities.

Anger becomes a problem when we involve the two extremes that are either overreacting or underreacting.

When we underreact, we repress or suppress our anger, often without realizing what we are doing. When we choose to block it out we are not being honest with ourselves or those around us. But when we overreact our anger is out of control. It comes out in rage and fury which can lead to violence. I have seen the dark blue bruises on faces and the wince when someone touches them. But that pain is minor compared to the inner emotional hurt which was experienced. Skin bruises eventually turn back to their normal color, but the inner discoloration lasts for much longer.

Let's explore some truths about anger. Hold on because what I am going to say may go contrary to what you have believed. Here they are:

"Anger is not the problem or the main emotion. Anger is a symptom!"

"Expressing your anger to your partner does not lessen your anger. It usually increases it!"

"How you use your anger was learned. This means you can learn a new response and get it under control."

"Your partner is not responsible for making you angry. You are!"

How do you feel now? Angry? Confused? Upset? Amazed? Let's consider these statements. And remember, what you do with the information in this chapter can have a dramatic affect on the amount of harmony and satisfaction you experience in your marriage.

Anger is what we call a secondary emotion. It's a message system telling you that something else is happening inside you.

Anger is caused by fear, hurt or frustration. That's right fear, hurt or frustration.

You may be afraid that your partner is going to override you, control you, yell at you, be unreasonable, not give you what you want, verbally attack you, withdraw, ignore you and so on. And to protect yourself from your fear you attack with anger. Whenever you begin to experience anger, ask yourself, "Is there something I am afraid of right now? What am I fearing?" You may discover the cause right at that moment. Try telling your partner, "I am somewhat fearful right now. Could we talk about it? I would rather do that than become angry."

Hurt! Hurt comes in many forms from a sharp word, being ignored, cooking a fine meal and having it passed over, painting the house and not receiving an appreciative comment, being slapped, discovering an affair and so on. To relieve our hurt we become angry. We want the other person to pay. We want to even the score but hurting people do not keep score in the same way. And each one continues the process of hurting. When we've been hurt, we don't always want to admit the extent of the hurt so we cover it over with anger.

When you are angry, ask yourself, "Am I feeling hurt? Where is this hurt coming from?" In place of your anger, try telling your partner, "Right now I am really feeling hurt. I wanted to let you know about it and talk about it and not have it develop into anger."

Frustration is at the heart of much of our anger. The word comes from the Latin *frustra,* which means "in vain." We are frustrated when we confront a problem, but can't find a solution for it. Frustration is the experience of walking into dead-end streets and blind alleys and getting nowhere. And a common myth is "frustration always has to upset us." It doesn't! If your partner is talking or acting in a way that bothers you, you may be frustrated, but you can control your response inwardly and outwardly. Many of your spouse's behaviors and reactions will not be what you want. They will annoy you but we all have the tendency to blow these out of proportion! We magnify what the other person has done and literally create a mountain out of a molehill.

There will be hundreds of little annoyances that can

activate your frustration button. But annoyances are part and parcel of married life. Accepting them and giving them permission to be there can relieve some of the pressure. Give your partner permission to talk the way he or she does, to do things differently, to be late, to be silent—and your frustration will lessen! Why? Because you have brought yourself back under control. We frequently become frustrated when we feel out of control.

Don't act aggressively when you become frustrated! This is a normal tendency but it's like blowing your horn at a train that has stopped in front of you, making you late. It's futile!

Remember, it isn't your partner who *makes* you angry. It's your inner response to the person that creates the anger. You and you alone are responsible for your emotions and reactions.

Let me be facetious for a minute and suggest how you can make yourself angry at your partner. It's quite easy. Just do the following. You are having a discussion with your spouse and you approach him or her with the attitude, "I *want* this and I *must* have it." The two key words are: "*want* and *must.*" The next step after not getting what you want is to say, "This is terrible. It's awful not to get what I want. Why don't you see it my way?" Then you say, "You shouldn't frustrate me like this. I must have my way. How dare you! You will pay for this!" And then the blame game begins. We assume that we must have our way and the frustration begins to build.

Janice shared with me an experience that happened just two days before her appointment with me. She described how she had spent six hours cleaning the house from corner to corner and top to bottom. She literally slaved over each room, making it spotless. She was hoping for some appreciation and response from her husband. Unfortunately, he came home tired, hungry and looking forward to the Monday night football game on TV. Not a word of appreciation was heard nor did he seem to notice. In fact, in a half hour he had undone much of her work in the family room by spreading himself and his stuff all over the furniture. We began talking about her thoughts which led up to the tirade and the big blow-up that lasted from 9:00 until 11:30 that night. Here is what she came up with:

"He should have noticed all the work I did today."
"He should have thanked me for what I did."
"He shouldn't have been so insensitive and inconsiderate."
"What a louse he is! He has no class or sensitivity!"
"Look at him! He messes up all my work!"
"He'll probably want sex tonight. Just wait. He'll pay for this and sleep by himself!"

We then talked about each statement and how it made her feel. Soon she began to see how the statements created hurt, frustration, rejection and then anger. The rest of the session was spent on developing some realistic responses to what had happened. As we brainstormed together about how to handle a disappointing experience, Janice began making a list. Here are some of the responses she could have used:

"I wish he would have noticed all of my work."
"I wonder why it is so important to have John notice the work and thank me for it? Did I do this for him or me or . . . ?"
"Perhaps I could find a creative way to share with him what I did today. I could bring in the camera and ask him if he would like to take a picture of a fantastically clean house and the housekeeper who created this wonder!"

We then formulated a summary statement which helped to put everything in perspective. It went like this: "I want John to notice the clean house that I've spent six hours slaving over today. But if he doesn't, that is all right, too. My happiness and sense of satisfaction does not depend on his response. I didn't clean it up just for his response. I cleaned it because it needed to be cleaned. I feel good about my effort and how it turned out. His appreciation would just be an added benefit."

I wonder what there is right now in your own life that would be helped by a response such as this. Perhaps there is a recent frustration that you could identify. Recall what you said to yourself and then formulate a new statement that would have lowered your frustration. It does work!

Do you know what this process actually does? It helps you put into practice some wisdom that can change your relationship with others. Consider these wise statements from Proverbs in the Amplified Version:

"He who is slow to anger has great understanding, but he who is hasty of spirit exposes and exalts his folly" (14:29).

"He who is slow to anger is better than the mighty, and he who relies on his own spirit than he who takes a city" (16:30).

"Good sense makes a man restrain his anger, and it is his glory to overlook a transgression or an offense" (19:11).

"Understand (this), my beloved brethren, let every man be quick to hear, slow to take offense and to get angry" (James 1:19, AMP).

As we see from these verses, not all anger is wrong. Ephesians 4:26 says, "Be angry and sin not!"

Write these verses on some three-by-five cards and keep them with you. Read them aloud several times each day for a month. By that time they will be yours! Then the Holy Spirit has the opportunity to bring them back to your conscious memory when you need them. Your responses can be consistent with the Word of God!

When you begin to experience anger, ask yourself, "What am I frustrated about? What am I doing to frustrate myself? Do I have some expectations or needs or wants that are not being met? Does my partner know what they are? And are they that necessary? Do I have to be frustrated at this time?" Take the time to answer these questions and it will make a difference in your life.

But let's consider the blame! Blame is the core issue of anger. You blame your partner when you find fault with what he or she has done and with the person. Blame means to accuse, point the finger at, find fault with, criticize, reproach, berate, disparage, chide, take to task and the list goes on.

Will blame accomplish what you want? Will blame bring you closer together? Will blame reflect the presence of Jesus Christ in your life and in your marriage? Yes, we want to make the other person aware of what they have done. Yes, we want them to pay for what they have done, but can they really? If we blame another person, that person may continue to do what he or she has done but with greater intensity. And if your partner is especially sensitive, he or she may begin to believe what you have said about him. Some of the worst statements and descriptions are those thrown at another person during the heat of anger. And some people end up believing what was said.

We blame others with the hope of correcting what they have done. How sad! How futile! How self-defeating! When you blame, you trigger your partner's defense system. This makes the person want to fight you and move into greater anger. If the justification process we use isn't working, then we think anger is the next best alternative. When you blame someone, you remain angry. It doesn't help it go away! And it distracts you from discovering a solution to your frustration.

Suggesting several other alternatives and solutions to the problem or conflict is better than blaming. The New Testament has something far better to offer than blame. It is called forgiveness. And it works. Forgiveness relieves us of the tremendous pressure of attempting to make others pay for what they have done to us. Even a spouse. Blame makes one ill. Forgiveness makes one well.

Earlier I mentioned that expression of your anger doesn't necessarily make it disappear. Let's look at the myths of "getting it out of your system." In many marital arguments we find the following scenario: The problem erupts, there is an angry outburst and verbal attacks which may include screaming and crying, exhaustion, a sullen apology and a strained relationship for several days. Is this helpful? Does it resolve the conflict? I'm not suggesting that we bottle up all our anger or repress it. But the way in which most individuals ventilate their anger does not make the anger disappear. Often by verbally expressing our anger at our partner we say things that are not easily forgotten. We are more concerned about proving the other person wrong or controlling him or even punishing him for what he said or did. What is the purpose of the expression of anger? To get rid of it?

There are numerous studies today which indicate the problem with expression of anger. An interesting study was conducted with divorced women to discover the cause of growth or stagnation. Two hundred and fifty-three women were interviewed twice—once during the upsetting time of divorce and then again four months later. Many questions were used to discover attitudes, reactions and so on. Questions about anger were asked such as: Did you show your anger or keep it in? Did you recover from it quickly or slowly? The results were surprising. The women who "let anger out" were *not* in better shape than those who "kept it in." Expressing anger did not automatically make a woman feel better, and it did not improve the woman's self-esteem. Those whose mental health improved were those who had an active social life following the divorce and *did not* harp on the divorce. Those who did not grow, socialized but tended to talk obsessively about the divorce.[2]

I am *not* suggesting that we should never talk about our anger or let it out. But let's choose a way to express it that will cause the anger to go away. Only then are we free from its tyranny over life and our marriage. Anger can be positive if it helps us solve the cause of anger. We need to communicate our anger without condemning! We need to express it in a way that reduces the anger and draws us closer to our partner. How is this done?

First, let's consider what you can do when your spouse is upset or angry with you. Remember, just because the other person is angry does not mean *you* have to become angry. Here are some suggestions:

Give your partner permission in your own mind to be angry with you. It is all right for him or her to be angry. It's not the end of the world and you can handle it without becoming a mirror reflection of it. Say the words to yourself, "It's all right for him/her to be angry. I can handle it."

Be sure you don't reinforce or reward your spouse for becoming angry with you. If the person yells, rants and raves, and stomps around and you respond by becoming upset or complying with what the person wants from you, guess what! You just reinforced your spouse's behavior. If your spouse is angry but reasonable, then respond by stating your point in a caring, logical manner. It also helps to reflect at that time what you hear your partner saying. Let your partner know that you can understand his or her being angry and upset at this time.

It's not wrong to ask your partner to respond to you in a reasonable manner. Suggest that your spouse restate the original concern, lower his or her voice and speak to you as though you had just been introduced for the first time.

Remember—if another person is angry, you do not have to become angry. This may be a good time to go back and read through the scriptures mentioned earlier. If anger interferes with the interaction between you and your spouse, there are ways you can change the pattern.

Identify the cues that contribute to the anger. It is important to determine how and when you express anger. What is it that arouses anger? What keeps the anger going? What is it that you do in creating the anger and keeping it going? Focus only on your part; don't lay any blame on your partner.

One way to accomplish this is by the use of a behavioral diary. Whenever anger occurs, each spouse needs to record the following:

1. The circumstances surrounding the anger, such as who was there, where it occurred, what triggered it, and so on.
2. The specific ways you acted and the statements you made.
3. The other person's reactions to your behaviors and statements.
4. The manner in which the conflict was eventually resolved (if at all).

Develop a plan of action for interrupting the conflict pattern. This plan should involve immediate action to disengage from the conflict. It should also be a way to face and handle the problem at a later time. Interrupting the conflict is an application of Nehemiah 5:6,7: "I [Nehemiah] was very angry when I heard their cry and these words. I thought it over, then rebuked the nobles and officials . . ." (AMP). This important principle to help resolve conflicts and create harmony is *delay.* When you begin to feel that anger is kicking open your emotional doors, delay any response. *Buy time.* And make use of the time by talking yourself down, using the principles in this chapter. You may find it beneficial to write out some responses you would rather use when angry. Practice them out loud so you can recall them when you become upset. It works.

Above all, memorize and practice the following questions. Using them as part of your delaying process will be constructive for both you and your partner.

1. Why am I angry? Am I experiencing hurt, rejection? Am I afraid? Am I frustrated? Over what? What are my unmet expectations, needs and wants?

2. What do I want at this time from this discussion with my spouse?

3. How can both of us get what we want? What is a better way to go about this?

Another positive step is to use neutral expressions such as, "I'm getting angry"; "I'm losing control"; "We're starting to fight"; or "I'm going to write out my feelings." Upon hearing one of these statements, the other person could say, "Thank you for telling me. What can I do right now that would help?"

A commitment from both of you not to yell or raise your voices and not to act our your anger is essential. We call this "suspending" the anger. Agree to return to the issue at a time of less conflict. Most couples are not used to taking the time to admit, scrutinize and then handle their anger.

The interruption period could be an opportune time for you to focus upon the cause of your anger.

David Mace suggests two additional positive ways to control your anger:

> This does not mean you do not have a right to be angry. In an appropriate situation, your anger could be a lifesaver. Anger enables us to assert ourselves in situations where we should. Anger exposes antisocial behavior in others. Anger gets wrongs righted. In a loving marriage, however, these measures are not necessary. My wife is not my enemy. She is my best friend; and it does not help either of us if I treat her as an enemy. So I say, "I'm angry with you. But I don't like myself in this condition. I don't want to want to strike you. I'd rather want to stroke you." This renouncing of anger on one side prevents the uprush of retaliatory anger on the other side, and the resulting tendency to drift into what I call the "artillery duel." If I present my state of anger against my wife as a problem I have, she is not motivated to respond angrily. Instead of a challenge to fight, it is an invitation to negotiate.
>
> Ask the other person for help. This step is the clincher. Without it, not much progress can be made. The anger may die down, but that is not enough. Both individuals need to find out

> just why one got mad at the other. If they do not, it could happen again, and again, and again. Your request for help is not likely to be turned down. It is in the other person's best interest to find out what is going on, and correct it if a loving relationship is going to be maintained.[3]

Anger will always be a part of even the healthiest of interpersonal relationships. The more intimate the relationship, the more possibility of hurt which can lead to anger. People are afraid of anger because of the fear of the hurt it can bring. Openly sharing your anger is different than being an angry person. Expressed in a healthy, noninsulting way, anger is acceptable. Anger expressed straight is better than anger camouflaged. I've seen some men and women who were so uneasy with their anger that it came out as laughter. It's usually a nervous laugh and then an attempt to withdraw from the other person. They're not comfortable with their own anger and cannot trust themselves enough to state how they are feeling factually. Much of the time their fear of expression is the fear of conflict.

Recently, I heard someone say that more marriages today are dying from silence than from violence. Silence. Repressed feelings. Coldness. Withdrawn emotions, but still alive and seething internally where they will do the greatest damage. How can you know what one another is feeling or thinking if the person is frozen like a dead iceberg? It's healthier to know than not to know. We need to feel our anger and then reveal it. When we're in control and express it properly, conflicts diminish.

When hurts have accumulated over a period of years in a marriage, the anger container is usually quite full and difficult to drain. I've often asked clients to take some paper and write a letter to their spouse (which will *not* be mailed) sharing with that person their feelings. This not only includes their anger but the original feelings that generated the anger. I suggest that after they have written this portion of the letter, they then write out what they really want from their relationship and suggest steps that could be taken to rebuild their closeness.

The last step is often the most difficult for it involves stating that you either forgive the other person or want to come to the place of forgiving him or her. Once the letter is completed the individuals have a choice of reading it out loud at home or bringing it to my office and reading it there to me. If they read it aloud at home, they go into a room, close the door and arrange two chairs facing each other. They sit in one and then assume their partner is in the other and read the letter to him or her. In either case, the process is a healthy draining experience which does not antagonize the other person. It's important to then consider what you will do the next time the problem arises so your anger will be in control and used in a healthy constructive manner.

Anger is a part of life and always will be because God created us with our emotions. But see your anger for what it is—a response to other feelings and remember . . . you *can* be in control. You can change!

Life-Changers

You can control your anger if you:

1. *Identify the true feeling behind your anger.*
2. *Apply God's Word to your anger.*
3. *Delay!*

God is at work within you, helping you want to obey him, and then helping you do what he wants. . . (Philippians 2:13 TLB).
No temptation has overtaken you but such as is common to man; and God is faithful who will not allow you to be tempted beyond what you are able, but with the temptation will provide the way of escape also, that you may be able to endure it (1 Corinthians 10:13).

12

The Breaking of a Vow

The class of eighty adults sat in stunned silence. No one was looking around. Each was concentrating on the speaker in front of the class, attempting to absorb what had just been said. Some were sure they had heard it correctly but others in their minds were saying, *Did I hear what I thought I just heard? Did he really say that?* Others sat in mild shock for the statement hit close to home.

The silence continued for a few more seconds until the speaker said, "Let me repeat what I just said to you. Most of you sitting here this morning have had an affair at one time or another during your marriage." The speaker slowly looked around the room at the various class members. Most of them were wondering what he would say next. Each person sat in rapt attention, eyes fixed on the speaker. Do you know what it is like to have eighty pair of eyes focusing upon you, wondering what you will say next? I do. I was the speaker that morning. I went on to say what I would point out to the readers of this book. Most couples have had an affair at one time or another in their marriage. *An affair is any outside event, activity or involvement which takes the time, energy and attention that rightfully belongs to the marriage relationship.*

People have affairs with their work, their hobbies, their

friends, their children, their church and so on. And these types of affairs often contribute to the creation of a physical affair with another person. When our mental energies and activities take priority over our partner, an affair is occurring. This outside factor is taking away from the exclusiveness of the marital relationship.

An affair brings intense pain, hurt and conflict into a marriage, but affairs often occur *because of* pain, hurt and conflict already existing within the marital relationship. The answer to conflict and dissatisfaction in marriage is not withdrawal and retreat to something or someone else. This only creates unfinished business in our lives. Affairs do not have to happen. There is a better way. But if an affair has occurred in any of these areas, healing is possible.

There are several categories of people who will read this chapter. Some of you have already been violated by the breaking of your marriage vows. Some of you have had the affair in your mind but never took the step of acting out the desire. Some of you will feel this chapter is not for you since it would *never* happen to you. Beware! Some of you may say, "I have never broken my marital vows," and this may be true. But your marriage has still been violated because of the lack of commitment, effort, time and energy to help your marriage become all that God wants it to be. Some of you are working on your marriage with a sincere desire for fidelity and purity.

Wherever you are and whoever you are—this chapter is for you.

Each year I counsel with numerous couples whose marriages have been shaken by an affair with another person. I say shaken in place of destroyed because the outcome does not have to be total destruction. The marriages that I have seen healed and restored give evidence to the grace of God and the power of Jesus Christ in a person's life. This healing is extensive, for an affair brings with it an intense pain involving the breaking of vows and trust, personal integrity, the burden of living a lie, the crumbling of one or both partners' self-esteem and the embarrassment of discovery. But affairs also hurt the cause of Jesus Christ and the ministry of the church. In our non-Christian society people are not shocked at the infidelity of the nonbeliever, but they do expect Christians to maintain a higher standard.

From the taking of marital vows in a church sanctuary in view of all the attendants and friends and relatives to the devastation of the discovery of the affair, what has happened? As so many partners who have become aware of their spouse's unfaithfulness express in our first meeting, "Why? Why did this happen? How could he or she do this? Why?"

There are reasons. There are answers. They will not take away the pain and the fact of what has happened. But knowing why affairs occur can help those who desire that fidelity be maintained from this point on in their marriage.

When you married your spouse, you *had* already been, for many years, married to a companion who will walk the road of life with you until the end. Each morning when you awaken and each night when you retire that companion will be right at your side.

This companion will never leave you for any reason. You can never sue this companion for nonsupport or separate maintenance. Divorce from this companion is an impossibility. Whether you like it or not, until death do you part is the vow placed upon you. This companion is temptation.

Everyone is tempted. I am tempted and you are tempted. Temptation knows no strangers. You cannot avoid it, evade it, escape it or kill it.

Along with death and taxes, it is a fact of life. You and I will stop being tempted only when the last breath of life flows from our bodies.

Some people have tried to escape temptation by cutting themselves off from other people. But it doesn't work. No one is exempt. Temptation is like a germ that is always in the body waiting to attack when one's resistance is lowered. People are tempted through the body and through the mind.[1]

Temptation begins in the mind. Therefore, affairs begin in the mind before they happen. Entertaining positive thoughts about another person can generate the growth of feelings which lead to further thoughts of *I wonder what it would be like . . . .* And then our bodies carry out the thoughts of the mind. Our mind creates the pictures which produce the fantasy that leads to an emotional response. This screams for release and the affair "just happened"! No marital partner can compete with the unrealistic pictures of a fantasy, for the comparison is totally unfair.

J. Allan Petersen describes the effect of the mind so well.

> The mind is a garden that could be cultivated to produce the harvest that we desire.
> The mind is a workshop where the important decisions of life and eternity are made.
> The mind is an armory where we forge the weapons for our victory or our destruction.
> The mind is a battlefield where all the decisive battles of life are won or lost.[2]

Yes—there are many reasons why affairs happen. They are not good or justifiable reasons, but they are the extension of a mind giving in to temptation.

Please remember that an affair is an indication that either the marriage or the person is in need of help. It's a warning that something is suffering.

> An affair can be welcome diversion from the burdens or boredom of a dull marriage.
> An affair occurs because of the desire to punish a spouse for what he or she has done.
> An affair occurs because of insufficient conscience development in a person.
> An affair occurs because of emotional immaturity which usually involves unresolved issues from the past.
> An affair occurs because of low self-esteem and the desire to be loved and valued by another person.
> An affair is an escape from the pressures of life.

The reasons are numerous but there are two major causes which we need to consider since they are directly related to the entire thrust of this book.

In the intimacy and closeness of marriage, conflicts are a natural result.

Therefore, *unresolved conflicts* are the breeding ground for the mind to cooperate with the temptations of life. Soon the fantasies and contact with someone else becomes the welcome diversion for an affair. The lie of an affair is that it will take away the pain of unresolved conflicts. In reality, however, it deepens and expands both the pain and the conflicts.

The battles which continuc in a marriage, whether large or small, soon lead to resentment—the feeling of ill will against another person with the accompanying feeling that the person must pay. And once resentment begins to play its song, rationalization begins to be the tune. "I deserve to be happy. I shouldn't be treated this way. Other people can make me happy. Spending time with that person is harmless. It's just a friendship." The statements continue and soon there is an involvement. I have listened to these statements scores of times.

The majority of conflicts occur because of unmet needs. Therefore, it follows that the majority of affairs occur because of *unmet needs!* The germ of temptation rejoices when needs are unmet for this opens the door for temptation to start to grow and spread. We marry for need fulfillment and when it doesn't happen, beware!

As Dr. James Dobson describes it:

> Great needs arise. The greater the needs for pleasure, romanticism, sex, and ego satisfaction, the greater the needs within marriage and the louder these voices scream. A need accumulates and is not being met. And the person is usually crying to others around them, "Meet my needs. Hear me. Love me. Understand me. Care for me." And these cries are not heard, understood, or responded to. We're at home, we're living together, but we're not meeting each other's needs. And the needs get louder; and when the needs get greater then the voices calling people into fidelity get greater.[3]

Sometimes unfulfilled needs come from confinement—not allowing one's partner to be who he or she really is. In a marriage our calling is to give our spouse the freedom to be himself or herself, to communicate his or her true feelings and to express his or her true needs. Our next task is to exhibit the servanthood model of marriage as described in Ephesians 5 and endeavor to meet the needs of that person.

Emotional deprivation in marriage is a major cause of an affair. The lack of need fulfillment and intimacy creates an intense vacuum. And this vacuum results in the breaking of marital promises. Promises? What promises? Your marital vows! They were promises to meet one another's needs and develop marital intimacy. Whenever there is an emotional affair (an affair of just the mind or feelings) or a physical affair, consider what is lacking in the relationship. However, I am not necessarily saying the "innocent" partner was to blame. I have seen a number of relationships in which one partner sincerely desired to met the needs of his or her partner and endeavored to do so, but the spouse had an insatiable need level or could not handle the fact that someone loved him or her that much. That sounds strange, but it does occur.

What are those basic unmet needs that, when combined with our thoughts and temptations, lead to an affair? Consider these.

> Affairs begin not just for sexual reasons but to satisfy the basic need we all have for closeness, goodness, kindness, togetherness—what I call the "ness" needs. When these needs are not met on a regular basis in a marriage, the motivation may be to find a person who will be good to us, touch us, hold us, give us a feeling of closeness. Sexual fulfillment may indeed become an important part of an extramarital relationship, but the "ness" needs are, for most men and women I know, initially more important.[4]

Affairs are a reaction to the marital vacuum. Every person, whether man or woman, has a need for attention. We want to be noticed for who we are and for what we do. We don't want to be taken for granted.

Acceptance is a basic need. We want to be accepted for who we are. If we try to remake our spouse into some unrealistic fantasy, we are trifling with the handiwork of God.

Affection needs must be met in marriage. That is one of the reasons you married. But this includes all types of affection including simple courtship responses as well as sexual fulfillment.

Admiration is a need whether you admit it or not. Both

women and men need this. Often a wife's sense of her own beauty depends not only on what her husband thinks of her but also what he verbalizes. Emotional nourishment comes from praise and compliments. Thinking positive thoughts about another person is the start, but these thoughts must be expressed for fulfillment to occur.

Charlie Shedd's practice of giving his wife at least one compliment a day over the past twenty-five years and one new compliment a week that he has never given before has validity!

The list can continue for page after page. What is most important is "Are you meeting your partner's needs? Is your partner meeting your needs?" Do you talk about your needs and express them in a way your partner understands? Go to your partner and say, "I care for you deeply and I never want either of us to ever become involved in an affair. It's important that I meet your needs and you meet mine. I need for you to let me know what yours are and what I can do to meet them and I will do the same for you. By doing this we will be better able to maintain our marital vows to one another through the grace of God!" I'm afraid that very few couples ever talked this honestly and openly. But why not? We must do so to maintain our commitment and marital vows.

I was moved by a poem written over a hundred years ago which conveys a feeling of the seriousness of marriage.

An Unfaithful Wife to Her Husband

Branded and blackened by my own misdeeds
I stand before you; not as one who pleads
For mercy or forgiveness, but as one,
After a wrong is done,
Who seeks the why and wherefore.

Go with me,
Back to those early years of love, and see
Just where our paths diverged. You must recall
Your wild pursuit of me, outstripping all
Competitors and rivals, till at last
You bound me sure and fast
With vow and ring.
I was the central thing
In all the Universe for you just then.

Just then for me, there were no other men.
I cared
Only for task and pleasures that you shared.
Such happy, happy days. You wearied first.
I will not say you wearied, but a thirst
For conquest and achievement in man's realm
Left love's barque with no pilot at the helm.
The money madness, and the keen desire
To outstrip others, set your heart on fire.
Into the growing conflagration went
Romance and sentiment.
Abroad you were a man of parts and power—
Your double dower
Of brawn and brains gave you a leader's place;
At home you were dull, tired, and commonplace.
You housed me, fed me, clothed me; you were kind;
But oh, so blind, so blind.
You could not, would not, see my woman's needs
Of small attentions; and you gave no heed
When I complained of loneliness; you said,
"A man must think about his daily bread
And not waste time in empty social life—
He leaves that sort of duty to his wife
And pays her bills, and lets her have her way,
And feels she should be satisfied."

Each day

Our lives that had been one life at the start,
Farther and farther seemed to drift apart.
Dead was the old romance of man and maid.
Your talk was all of politics or trade.
Your work, your club, the mad pursuit of gold
Absorbed your thoughts. Your duty kiss fell cold
Upon my lips. Life lost its zest, its thrill,

Until

One fateful day when earth seemed very dull
It suddenly grew bright and beautiful.
I spoke a little, and he listened much;
There was attention in his eyes, and such
A note of comradeship in his low tone,
I felt no more alone.
There was a kindly interest in his air;
He spoke about the way I dressed my hair.
And praised the gown I wore.

It seemed a thousand, thousand years and more
Since I had been noticed. Had mine ear
Been used to compliments year after year,
If I had heard you speak
As this man spoke, I had not been so weak.
The innocent beginning
Of all my sinning
Was just the woman's craving to be brought
Into the inner shrine of some man's thought.
You held me there, as sweetheart and as bride;
And then as wife, you left me far outside.
So far, so far, you could not hear me call;
You might, you should, have saved me from my fall.
I was not bad, just lonely, that was all.

A man should offer something to replace
The sweet adventure of the lover's chase
Which ends with marriage. Love's neglected laws
Paves pathways for the "Statutory Cause."[5]

There are numerous books today which deal with the subject of affairs. Many have chapters dealing with the aftermath of an affair. There are various steps to take to bring about healing in the marriage after an affair and a positive outcome to a very painful experience. Three such resources are *How to Save Your Marriage from an Affair* by Dr. Ron Edell (Kensington Publishers), *The Myth of the Green Grass* by J. Allan Petersen (Tyndale), Chapters 6–8, and *Seasons of a Marriage* by this author (Regal Books).

There is one overlooked ingredient, however, that can help us maintain fidelity. That is the constant renewal of our wedding vows. I don't mean necessarily the ones we shared at the wedding, since most people hardly remember what they said anyway. I do mean an amplification of those vows as our understanding of wedding vows and our commitment to one another deepens.

If I were to ask you to put this book down and go to your partner and restate your wedding vows, could you? And if you said you would "Forsake all others and love, honor and cherish your partner until death do you part," do you really know what that means?

Humanly speaking, marriage vows are difficult to keep. One reason is that at the time of marriage, most adults really have no idea of what they are committing themselves to.

Some of the most profound thoughts on marriage that I have ever read come from a book titled *The Mystery of Marriage:* "To keep a vow . . ." Mike Mason writes, "means not to keep from breaking it, but rather to devote the rest of one's life to discovering what the vow means, and to be willing to change and to grow accordingly."[6] *Is this occurring in your marriage at the present time?* Many of us believe that love is the glue that holds marriage together. But consider another and better possibility.

> So while love must certainly be present if a marriage is to continue and be successful, practically speaking, it is the vows which really hold the thing together, undergirding love itself. Of course, this is just another way of saying that love is not an emotion or an experience, but a promise, a resolve, an act of the will.
>
> Marriages which are dependent on love fall apart, or at best are in for a stormy time of it. But marriages which consistently look back to their vows, to those wild promises made before God, and which trust Him to make sense out of them, find a continual source of strength and renewal. We must return to an attitude of total abandonment, of throwing all our natural caution and defensiveness to the winds and putting ourselves entirely in the hands of love by an act of the will. Instead of falling into love, we may now have to march into it.[7]

How quickly we forget our promises and give little regard to our vows. God calls us to be people of our word, to be faithful in our promises and pledges, not to stagnate and remain with limited marital vows. For the longer we are married, the more we come to realize that our understanding of vows means we need to add to them periodically. By doing this we create a basis for handling the disturbances and conflicts of marriage as well as building toward the prevention of infidelity.

If you were to rewrite your wedding vows at this time, what would you say? What would you commit and promise to do? What is needed in terms of an expanded commitment for your marriage? Before you read on, take a few minutes and write down what you would like your vows to include. Ask your partner to do the same. Discuss them together. I would like to see an added dimension to the celebration of the yearly wedding anniversary. I would like to see each couple take time to expand upon their wedding vows each year and either verbally or in writing share these with one another. In this way, each would be reminded of his or her commitment before God.

We are people who easily forget and need to be reminded. The children of Israel in the Old Testament were given signs and customs to remember. There is so much interference with marriage today by our complex society, we must fight to make it a priority for the glory of God. Here are some vows other people have written to their partner. What would you write?

"My commitment to you is to listen to your concerns each day for the purpose of having the kind of marriage we both want."

"I realize that our love will change and I will work to maintain a high level of romance, courtship and love in our relationship."

"I pledge myself to confront problems when they arise and not retreat like a turtle into my shell."

"I commit myself to you in times of joy and in times of problems. We will tackle and share our problems together."

"I commit myself to backing you up with your discipline of the children and I ask the same of you."

"I promise that I will never be too busy to look at the flowers with you."

"I will respect your beliefs and capabilities which are different from mine and will not attempt to make you into a revised edition of me."

"I will accept the confinements of marriage and giving up of some freedoms. I accept that this can help me grow and I will not fight my new restrictions."

"I will be open and honest with no secrets and I desire you to be the same with me."

One last thought about your vows:

The marriage vows give glory to God. While it is true that a man and a woman on their wedding day take a step toward a unique fulfillment of the commandment of love, it is even more true to say of matrimony that it is a sacramental outpouring of God's grace enabling such love to take place. The human couple indicates humbly a willingness to give themselves to this love; but it the Lord Who makes love possible in the first place, and therefore it is He Who promises that His gift of love will not be taken away.

Therefore, anyone who has taken these vows (assuming they have been taken in good faith) need no longer worry about "falling out of love." For we have vowed not to. Nor will there be any justification for anxiety over the possibility of our loved one getting fat, ugly, sick, growing old, being unable to work anymore, or doing something evil or shameful. For we have vowed to continue loving in spite of all changes and adversity, in spite of good times, bad times, wealth, or poverty. In making such reckless promises we have freely admitted that we ourselves cannot keep them, yet equally freely have we confessed our unreserved faith in and dependence upon the God Who can, the God Whose very nature is expressed in faithfulness, that is, in the keeping of apparently impossible promises to His people.[8]

Life-Changers

Each day renew your vow of fidelity and your commitment to meet one another's needs.

Each day resubmit your heart and mind to God who makes it possible to fulfill your marital vows.

Therefore, encourage one another, and build up one another, just as you also are doing (1 Thessalonians 5:11).

13

"I Believe in You"

Arthur sat in the chair in my office for several minutes looking disgusted. I had asked him a question and was wondering why he wasn't responding. His wife sat in the other chair waiting for him to say something. A minute before she had broken the silence by saying, "That's just what he does at home. He sits and doesn't say anything."

"Well, let's give Art all the time he wants," I replied. "There's no hurry."

Finally he said, "I'll tell you why I don't say anything. I've given up. I feel beaten down. When I do say something, it's never right. Most of what I hear is criticism and negatives. I would give anything right now for a word of encouragement and for someone . . . to believe in me and give me the benefit of the doubt."

How many times have I heard that statement? How many times have you either heard it or said it yourself? It's a cry of desperation—a need for encouragement that all of us have. Believing in another person means that we encourage the person, give the person the benefit of the doubt and think the best of him or her.

If you would like to prevent conflicts and lessen the tension and pain in your marriage, encourage! It's so easy to be a critic, but so much more rewarding to be an encourager. When you criticize you stand *against* your spouse. When you encourage, you stand *beside* your spouse. It's better to live in a humble environment of encouragement than in a castle filled with criticism.

I've asked many people how they felt encouragement from others. This is what some of them have said:

"She understood my feelings even when it was hard to share them."
"He listens to me. I mean really listens and doesn't interrupt or criticize."
"My husband sees me as a winner. He says I am special."
"My husband takes time for me and says no to his work."
"He keeps telling me I can do it even when I don't feel I can. It's made all the difference in the world."
"She lets me explain first instead of giving me her opinion. And she believes me."
"A friend of mine shared his hope and faith with me when mine was gone. I needed that, to believe in me."
"My parents cheered me on in life."

The word "encourage" means "to give courage to another person." It means "to inspire with courage, to give spirit or hope, hearten, spur on, stimulate." The Hebrew term for encourage conveys the idea of putting strength into someone's hands, arms or body so they can handle pressure. That's a big order. But in contrast the word discourage means "to deprive of courage, to dishearten, to hinder, to deter."

Encouragement comes from a heart of caring and love and is conveyed through words, attitudes and actions. Recently I heard the statement that "Words that encourage are inspired by love and directed toward fear." That's an interesting concept.

There are so many times when your words to your partner will be the deciding factor . . . in either direction! Will it be discouragement that cripples or encouragement that inspires? Words of encouragement heal conflicts and hurts. Proverbs 12:18 states, "There is one who speaks rashly like the thrusts of a sword, but the tongue of the wise brings healing." The Living Bible says, ". . . the words of the wise soothe and heal." First Thessalonians 5:11 states, "Therefore encourage one another, and build up one another, just as you also are doing."

But how does encouragement relate to conflicts in a

marriage? *When a partner feels an attitude of encouragement and belief coming from his or her spouse, the person will usually be open, vulnerable and willing to look at issues in order to resolve them!* It works. I have seen it work with clients and with my own personal relationships for years. But I'm sure your question may be, "How? How do I encourage? What is the best way to encourage?"

Encouraging your partner is the process of believing in that person. You focus on his or her resources to build that person's self-esteem, self-confidence and feelings of worth. You help the person see himself as God sees him. You can focus in on any of your partner's resources. You can also take traits which you feel might be liabilities and discover the positive side of what may have been a "pain in the neck." You're a talent scout seeking to discover the underdeveloped potential in that person. Too often we find it easier to respond to the finished product in a person rather than the raw undeveloped potential. But what excitement can occur as you see a person develop, change and grow! Our calling in marriage is not to be a blockage but a blockage-breaker. Most of us have been conditioned to be aware of people's mistakes and liabilities. It may help us feel better about our own imperfections. But it's not very pleasant living in a mistake-oriented environment.

You see, if you encourage your partner, your spouse will relax and because *of you* develop some confidence which he or she never felt before. Realistically, *expect the best from your spouse.*

When your partner is having a difficult time and is despairing, you can encourage him or her by pointing out a capability or strength which that person may be overlooking. Focus on the effort or attempt he or she makes in a difficult situation.

You can encourage as much through your nonverbal communication as through what you actually say. Encouragers are listeners.

Here are some of the phrases that are used to encourage others:

"You're really capable."
"I realize you're struggling with that, but give it a try."

"Yes, sometimes it's hard for us to talk about our differences, but I appreciate what you've been trying. I will listen to you."

"If you made a mistake, then you learned. I'd like to know what you learned."

"Honey, do it at your pace and not mine. It's all right for us to have different clocks inside us."

"Just give it your best shot. That will be great."

Before you consider how you encourage your spouse, how do you encourage yourself? Strange question? Not at all. It's difficult to encourage others if you haven't learned to treat yourself well. You've got to be happily married to yourself before you can be happily married to another person. Before you start with your spouse, let's start with you. Complete the following lists.

I. List six of your developed strengths or capabilities.

II. Now list two encouraging comments you make to yourself about each of these strengths.

III. Let's consider your undeveloped capabilities and potential strengths. Make a list of these.

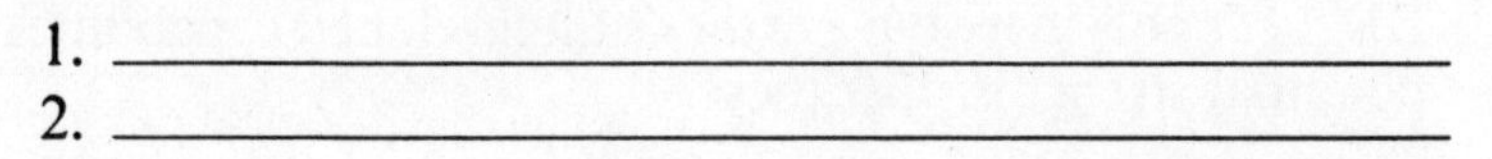

3. ______________________
4. ______________________
5. ______________________
6. ______________________

IV. What encouraging comments could you make to yourself that would enable you to develop these further? List six of these.

1. ______________________
2. ______________________
3. ______________________
4. ______________________
5. ______________________
6. ______________________

Now it's time to consider your partner.

I. Make a list of six of his or her developed strengths or capabilities.

1. ______________________
2. ______________________
3. ______________________
4. ______________________
5. ______________________
6. ______________________

II. List the encouraging comments you make to your partner about these strengths or capabilities.

1. ______________________
2. ______________________
3. ______________________
4. ______________________
5. ______________________
6. ______________________

III. Let's consider your partner's undeveloped capabilities and potential strengths. List these.

IV. What kind of encouraging comments could you make to your partner which would enable him or her to develop these strengths further? List at least six of these.

Now that you've made your list, it's not over. What will you do with these comments for yourself and for your spouse? How often will you share them? When will you begin? How will you continue to be a consistent encourager? Write out your plan in the space provided.

____

____

____

____

____

____

Encouragement carries with it the message that, "You're O.K." and "I believe in you." Your messages can be sent by mail, phone calls, Federal Express, telegrams, smoke signals as well as by hugs, pats on the back or shoulder, a playful wink, a thumbs-up sign or a verbal compliment. Some responses simply recognize the other person's presence. Too basic? Not at all. I hear complaints of, "He comes home, grunts at me, looks through the mail, throws his coat on the chair and goes to the TV. He never even stops walking. I'd just like to be recognized as a human. I'd like him to acknowledge that I exist and that I'm his wife, *not* the hired hand!"

A man in one of my seminars complained that when he walked in the door he rarely ever got a hello. But the dog would come running in, jump up and down, lick his hand, roll over for its stomach to be rubbed and wag its tail furiously. He shared this in front of thirty-five couples and before I could respond one of the other men in the group piped up and said, "You want your wife to do all that, too?" The laughter drowned out any response that I could give.

Funny but true. It might not be such a bad idea after all. Encouragement means not taking your partner for granted. Your partner is a unique gift to you who needs constant recognition and maintenance. It's important to be committed to your marriage, but it's just as important to be committed to your spouse. Many spouses suffer from emotional malnutrition because of too little encouragement.

Some encouragement responses will enhance your spouse's sense of self-worth: "You're special to me, I am so glad I married you"; "I love you more each day." Say it while looking intently at your partner.

There are other encouraging comments which are based upon your partner's performance or competency: "Boy, you're a great cook. Keep it up"; "I like the way you've decorated the house. Your ideas are excellent."

Other statements express appreciation which tend to reinforce what it was that you liked: "Thanks for remembering my favorite dessert. That made my day for my stomach"; "Thanks for stopping by the post office and picking up that certified letter. It sure saved me some time"; "Thanks for ironing my shirts and having them ready for me each day. That's a lot of help and comfort."

We all need a combination of encouraging statements for both *doing* and *being*. Statements like, "You're a classy person," or "I care deeply for you," or "I like you just for who you are as a person" are *being* statements. *Doing* encouragements are easy to give and are quite common: "Thank you for doing . . ." It's important to give and receive both, but our tendency is to give more encouragement based on doing. Unfortunately, since so many people today build their sense of self-esteem on their performance and accomplishments, it tends to reinforce this trend. It can also leave some spouses feeling that they are appreciated just for their being a great task completer. Be creative!

There are verbal and nonverbal expressions of encouragement. A smile, a hug, a touch, a wink, a wave, a thumbs-up sign are great expressions. Which are most important to your partner? Do you know? Have you asked? Go ahead, ask. You may know but so often spouses do not know, they just assume. Why ask? Because all of us speak a different language and this includes our love language as well as our language of encouragement. Some spouses thrive on verbal encouragement. They love to be told. Others put touching and hugs—or even winks—at the top of their priority list.

Some prefer *being* statements whereas others prefer *doing* responses. And by receiving both it's possible to learn to value both as well. You may not feel encouraged by your partner and your partner may not feel encouraged by you. And both of you think, "Why doesn't my partner feel encouraged? I *do* encourage him but it doesn't seem to register!" That may be true and the reason it doesn't register is that you're not sharing it in his language!

Your partner may do a lot for you, but you prefer verbal *being* responses. On the other hand your partner may simply appreciate more of the nonverbal. You may be giving expressions of encouragement that you like, but these are not what register with your partner. Learn to speak your partner's language of encouragement. Let him or her know what and how you like to be encouraged as well. Each of you make a list and exchange lists. Share with each other your responses to the questions listed earlier in this chapter. Ask each other how you prefer being encouraged in public as well as at home. There may be a difference.

Sensitivity to what another person needs is a gift to ask for from the Lord. Your answer may come through what your partner shares with you or at times of upset or distress. Or God may speak to you directly and give you that wisdom.

John was a young man who had experienced several weeks of pressure and stress. He was having difficulties at work with schedules and some unreasonable demands from the company. And since John and his wife had moved several hundred miles from his parents, mom and dad were very unhappy and in various ways were letting him know about it. In addition, a small investment which he had made had just gone sour and John learned about this on a particularly bad day.

When he arrived home, John's nonverbals just seemed to shout discouragement and dejection. He felt, as he said later, "Shattered. I felt like I was in small pieces and really felt like a total failure that day." When he came home, he slumped in a chair and said very little. John never expressed his feelings verbally very much, but the discouragement showed. When his wife Jane came into the room she read his body language and knew it had not been a particularly good day. She seemed to know just what to do. She came up behind him and stood gently stroking his hair and massaging his drooping shoulders. She asked the typical questions such as, "What's wrong?" or "Do you want to talk about it?" or "Would you feel better if you talked about it?"

"Her touch," as John said, "lifted me out of the pit better than anything she could have said. At times talking helps, but for her to know that I didn't need words but just encouragement through her touch made me a whole man again. That was great! I hope I can learn to be that sensitive." What could have become a conflict became a time of encouragement.

I heard a unique story of an act of encouragement which occurred at a very upsetting time. In fact, it was a preventative act of shielding a spouse from a very embarrassing situation. And it was so encouraging to the wife to know that her husband would shield her in that way.

Susan and Hank had been invited to one of the adult class potluck dinners and this was their first social event since coming to the church. She had been asked to bring a pie for dessert which was a bit threatening because she and Hank knew that cooking wasn't one of her gifts. But she decided to go ahead and make a chocolate custard pie. As they started driving to the party, she became really concerned because they both smelled the overcooked crust and scorched custard. When they turned the corners in the car, she could feel the custard move about in the pie shell a bit too much. Then panic began to set in, but it was too late to drop by the store and buy anything.

They arrived at the home and placed her dessert on the hostess table with all the other dishes. She quickly cut two small pieces and gave one to Hank and she ate the other. They both realized they had a disaster on their hands! "Don't worry," Hank said, "I'll take care of this."

After everyone had eaten their salad and main course and before anyone else headed for the dessert table, Hank went over, picked up the pie, and announced to the guests that since there were so many desserts and his wife rarely had a chance to make his favorite pie, he planned to eat her pie alone and make a pig of himself. He joked about it and the others responded with their imitations of a pig and he sat down.

Susan said she "couldn't believe it. Hank sat there by himself mashing up the inedible pieces and eating the rest so no one else would know how bad it was. I felt so relieved by what he did and so secure. In fact, I took him out to a restaurant the next week that had a dessert buffet so he could enjoy his desserts." What could have become conflict became a time of encouragement.

Recently, I heard of another couple, Jenny and Tom, who attended a social function with a number of other couples and overheard the conversation of two of their friends. The wife was a bit discouraged about some new concerns at her job and questioned her ability to handle them. She shared this with some of her friends at the gathering and her husband responded several times with encouraging comments and the belief that she had the capability to handle the job. He also reflected that he could understand her concerns and helped her express her feelings even more.

As Jenny and Tom drove home there was silence for awhile and then Jenny asked her husband if he had overheard the conversation of their friends. He said yes he did.

"Did you hear how he encouraged her?" Jenny asked.

"Yes, I did," Tom replied. "And I was impressed by that, too."

A few seconds of silence went by and then Jenny said in a soft voice, "I wish you would encourage me like that at times. It would mean a lot to me."

Tom replied with an interesting comment: "I would like to, but very honestly there are so many times when I just don't know what to say. It would help me if you would write out several statements that you would like me to make and I will be glad to learn to encourage you."

How do you respond to what Tom said? Should Jenny have to write these out for him or should he learn to figure them out for himself? Is this a healthy approach? Some wives would say, "I'm sorry. I don't want you memorizing a list of what I've suggested. I want you to do some creative thinking on your own." That is one way of looking at Tom's response. But I believe there is a healthier and more encouraging way to respond.

There are many men today who were raised without a male model of encouragement and they really do not know what to say. To admit his deficit and ask for help are positive steps for Tom. In time, I think he will come up with his own comments and add some variety to his response. To receive the proper encouragement we may need to become a playwright and create a script for the other player. It is actually quite simple. By doing this you are showing how much you value the comments of your partner. Here are some examples:

A husband has worked hard for several hours in the yard in 90 degree weather. He doesn't hear any response from his wife as she walks through the yard and looks around. He says in a cheerful voice, "I'd really like to hear how you like the yard. That would replace the gallon of my sweat that is soaking up the ground."

A wife who cooked dinner each night with her husband's needs in mind rarely heard any compliments. She said, "Honey, it would help me to hear that you enjoyed the dinner and appreciate the work that went into it. From the smile on your face and the contented groan, I think you liked it, but I really enjoy hearing from you in my language."

What kind of script would you write? What kind would your spouse create? Why not ask each other? Issues that could be conflicts can become times of encouragement.

Encouragement takes many forms of expression. In fact, the one I would like to encourage you to consider now is very different. This form is having faith in your partner and giving him or her the benefit of the doubt. We all need someone to trust and believe in us, even when there is not always much that may be believable because of past experience. First

Corinthians 13:7 says, "Love gives the other person the benefit of a doubt" (AMP). It means taking one's spouse at his or her word and re-interpreting his or her characteristics and behaviors to see the positive side.

Those who tend to be perfectionistic, precise, detailed and highly organized may have some difficulty with the area of tasks, however. Have you ever asked your partner to do something and then checked up on him to see if he did it before he's had a chance to do it or before it was due? This may come as a surprise, but being a "checker-upper" is not a spiritual gift. We encourage one another by believing in the fact that a task given will mean a task completed.

Now you're saying, "But you don't know my spouse and how many times he hasn't followed through." That may be true, but approaching him in a new manner with proper timing, using his language, getting his attention, even helping him with his plans to follow through, and then believing in him will bring it about! Your not asking, your silence, your patience says, "I believe in you. I believe you can do it." It shows encouragement and will certainly eliminate some of your conflicts. Just remember, by *not* believing in the person and checking up on him, you will probably create the very problem you want to avoid! So many people have sat in my office and said, "Well, I'll ask him/her to do this. But I really doubt if he or she will carry through." And, with a hurt or angry expression, the partner will turn to me and say, "See? See what I've been saying? Why should I even try? There's no belief or trust in me. That's why I want out of this marriage. Fifteen years of this is enough!"

Are you an "It's impossible. It will never work" type of person? Or are you a Caleb and Joshua in the Old Testament who said, "We can do it"? When the twelve spies came back from their venture into the promised land, there was a difference in response. Chuck Swindoll described it so well. "Ten saw the problem; two saw the solution. Ten saw the obstacles; two saw the answers. Ten were impressed with the size of the men; two were impressed with the size of their God. Ten focused on what could not be accomplished; two focused on what could easily be accomplished by the power of God."[1]

Sometimes we are like the ten when it comes to believing in another person. But the response of Caleb and Joshua works as we view people just as it worked for the acquisition of the promised land. Are you with the ten or the two?

Encouragement means you believe your spouse is going to respond differently even though his or her past track record is not that positive.

Sheri and her husband were sitting in my office, and we were talking about their pattern of communication. Sheri was saying, "I can tell from his short, terse comments and his scowls that he's upset with me and when I ask him, 'What's wrong?' and I get, 'Nothing is wrong.'"

I turned to Tony and asked, "What should Sheri do when she senses something is wrong?"

"Just ask me," Tony replied.

"But she said she does and you say nothing! Something is usually wrong, isn't it?"

Tony answered, "Yes, I'm usually upset about how she's getting after the kids."

"Why not share how you're feeling since you show it anyway?" I turned to Sheri and said, "Just ask him each time, 'What's wrong?'"

Sheri started to counter with, "But all I've gotten in the past is . . ." but I interrupted.

"Could you tell Tony what he will be hearing in the future?"

She caught on (since we had been talking about believing in the other person). So she said, "Tony, when I sense that something is wrong, I will ask you and I believe that from now on you will be more open to telling me what's wrong. And each time you do I will thank you for telling me."

"That would be great," Tony said. "I can handle that. And I sure like hearing from you that you believe I'll be different. I will tell you what I'm feeling and even if I don't know what I'm feeling, I'll tell you that to. But don't criticize my feelings like you've done in the . . ."

I interrupted, "Tony tell Sheri what you believe she will do in the future."

"You're right," he said. "I was going to condemn Sheri before anything ever happened because of what's happened before. Sheri, I believe that when I share my feelings you'll listen, thank me and then we can work toward a solution."

This exchange happens quite often in counseling and this is what I mean by believing in the other person and trusting that he or she will change. How could you express this belief to your partner?

How do you show another person that you are giving him or her the benefit of the doubt? One other way is to re-interpret what you have labeled as negative. Often what appears negative is an approach or characteristic that is different from our own. We tend to label behavior or beliefs or attitudes in an attempt to show the people we feel they're wrong. This also implies that we want them to change. Labeling a behavior as negative rarely encourages a person to change. Rather, we tend to dig in our heels and remain the same way.

You do have a choice in terms of how you view any situation and how you respond to your partner's behavior. Yes, you may have some situations in your marriage that you consider negative, but you can discover a new way of viewing them and thus give your partner "the benefit of the doubt." Here are a few examples.

Your spouse leaves quite early for work and doesn't wake you to tell you goodbye. If this is not his/her normal pattern, you could feel slighted and ignored. *How can you relabel this to give your spouse the benefit of the doubt?* Your spouse was being considerate by letting you sleep longer and not disturbing you.

Your spouse gets up early each morning to exercise before leaving for work. You hear your spouse each morning and are disturbed by the noise. You get a bit angry since it seems inconsiderate. *How can you relabel this to give your spouse the benefit of the doubt?* You have a spouse who is concerned about his health enough to keep in shape. This is something to be pleased about.

One could label one's spouse as a liberal person or broad-minded and fair to all. We could label him quiet or one who measures his words carefully and puts ample thought behind his statements. We could label a very verbal person as over-talkative or we could label her as friendly. We can label a person as argumentative or simply someone who loves a good, lively discussion.

It's your choice what you label a person—but remember that we label people from our own perspective and background. Someone else may not attach that label to the person at all!

A stubborn person could be called persistent and determined. A talkative person is informative and friendly. A noisy person is inquisitive and concerned. Encouraging means taking what you label a liability and turning it into an asset. What a delight it is to look for new ways to encourage others. Pull out all the stops. Try it intensely for one month. There will be changes! We are encouraged people because of what God has done for us through His Son. Let's share this gift with our partner.

Life-Changers

Be a courage-giver.

Expect the best from your partner and give him or her the benefit of the doubt.

Encourage for "being" and "doing."

Let all bitterness and wrath and anger and clamor and slander be put away from you, along with all malice. And be kind to one another, tender-hearted, forgiving each other, just as God in Christ has forgiven you (Ephesians 4:31–32).

14

Let Loose of Your Hurt

Have you ever been to the Grand Tetons—those majestic mountains rising thousands of feet from the floor of Jackson Hole with their ragged terrain and year-round glacial patches looking something like the Swiss Alps? Over the past nineteen years Joyce and I have been there fifteen times. It's our favorite place to be refreshed and enjoy a dramatic reminder of God's handiwork. We've fished, hiked numerous trails and areas where no trails existed, floated the Snake river, and waded the various streams in search of beautiful cutthroat trout.

One morning we put on our day packs and started up the trail to Bradley Lake. We walked the two miles up the sloping paths and when we arrived we were fresh and rested. We had limited the number of items we carried with us so the weight of our packs wouldn't become a wearisome burden. We wanted to walk at a brisk pace, enjoy the surroundings and have energy when we arrived.

Arriving about 9:00 in the morning, we left the trail and walked through the wet grass into the last small strand of trees. We emerged from the woods to find ourselves on level ground adjoining the lake. From there we proceeded to the sand bar. Taking off our day packs and coats, we put the finishing touches on our fishing equipment and went to work. I let the line drift into the current of the small stream at the inlet of the lake; the natural force and pull of the stream took out line. A few seconds later a violent pull vibrated up the length of the pole. The battle was on. Joyce was as excited as I was. A minute later we would see a seventeen-inch reddish brown cutthroat trout coming through the clear water.

Landing that first fish was just the start of a delightful morning for the two of us. We hiked through forest and meadows, climbed over downed trees, scrambled over rough shorelines and waded through shallow water. Along the way we saw numerous rocks and pieces of driftwood that we would have liked to take back with us. We began picking up some unusual rocks and pieces of wood. But as we continued we realized that we were becoming absorbed with collecting. I had limited how far we were going to be able to explore and travel. Our day packs would not be able to contain all that we were thinking of collecting. We also thought about how exhausted we would be carrying all this back to our car. A wise decision was made. We put it all back where we found it. It belonged there and not with us.

Our hike back around the lake was pleasant and not a burden. Had we taken what we thought we needed, our attention would have been upon the weight of what we had collected as it rested more and more heavily upon our shoulders. It would have distracted us from the beauty of the clear skies, paintbrush and columbine, and the gentle wind whispering through the pine and aspen trees. It was a day to remember.

Many individuals and couples carry a weight around with them unnecessarily. This keeps them from experiencing life to its fullest. Some are collectors. They collect excess emotional baggage which acts as an anchor hindering both progress and direction.

Some people collect garbage. Some collect stamps. Some collect records and fine art. And some collect hurts!

Conflicts carry with them the potential for raw wounds and hurts, many of which have difficulty healing over a period of time. Some people feel the pang of pain every day, for their wounds are open to the air. Others bury their hurts and wounds as their way of diminishing the reminder of the pain. Burying does not kill the pain. Instead, while it is buried it feeds and grows and becomes even more painful when it rises to catch a breath of fresh air.

Many of the hurts which we experience we never deserved.

During conflict between married partners, words are exchanged which penetrate and sometimes change the partner. Some words are like arrows: they enter the victim and when the shaft of the arrow is pulled free, the jagged point remains to fester and keep the hurt alive. If you've been hurt by your partner for one reason or another, I'm sure you've wished you could reach back to that painful encounter and cut it out of your life.

We are all different in the way we handle our hurts. One spouse holds the hurt for weeks and months while the other seems to relinquish it in hours. Dr. Lewis Smedes put it well when he said:

> Some people are lucky; they seem to have gracious glands that secrete the juices of forgetfulness. They never hold a grudge; they do not remember old hurts. Their painful yesterdays die with the coming of tomorrow. But most of us find that the pains of our past keep rolling through our memories, and there's nothing we can do to stop the flow.[1]

Kim responded in counseling one day with a strong outburst: "I can't believe Jack. We fight and quarrel and never seem to resolve the problem. He is so stubborn. He can never bring himself to say he's sorry or that he's the one who's wrong. Then in an hour he wants to get close and cozy. I'm still smarting from what he said. I just can't get over it that fast and he doesn't understand. I don't think he cares as much as I do or he wouldn't get over it that fast. It takes me days and sometimes weeks. And I've been hurt so much lately, I'm getting to the place where I wonder if I can ever really forgive him."

An unusual outburst? No, for many feel the same way. When someone has been offended there is a lingering hurt. I work with a number of people who are consumed with bitterness and resentment. Ephesians 4:31 tells us to put away all bitterness. Bitterness is the disposition of a person with a tongue sharp as an arrow. He "needles" others and is ready with a sharp and painful reply to his spouse. Resentment is that feeling of ill will toward a person which wants the person to make an on-going series of payments for what he or she has done to us.

The problem with being bitter and resentful is that we

have allowed what our spouse has said or done to control our emotions and our lives. If we do not release our spouse from whatever wrong he or she has done, we simply enslave ourselves to the hurt in our past. Being chained to hurt and hate from the past means anger and resentment in our future. When we hold onto our hurts we are misusing the gift of memory. We are choosing to use our memory to hurt as we have been hurt. How? By keeping the hurt alive and in some way perhaps plotting to hurt in return. We use memory as a weapon.

I remember years ago seeing a Western movie in which two antagonists looked at each other from thirty feet away clutching their weapons which had the power to kill their opponent. But at the same time, both of them abandoned their weapons, and said, "I will fight no more. There never is a real winner. We've tried fighting. Let's try living." And with that they moved toward each other in peace. When we abandon the hurt it means even when we become upset with our partner (and we will) the past hurt will *never* be mentioned again or used to punish, manipulate or embarrass our spouse. That is no longer an option. Life will always be full of unfairness and hurt. That's the way it is. Forgiveness seems unfair for by forgiving, we are freeing the other person from payment. That's true. That's the way it must occur if we are to find healing for our hurts.

"But," you say, "if I forgive my partner for what she said, she could do it again." True! That's the way it is.

"If I forgive my partner, I make myself vulnerable and open to being hurt again." True! That's the way it is. But it's still the best alternative to being frozen in hurt because of disagreement. If you want your partner to pay and you withhold love and affection, use silence, are blunt, cold or caustic, when is the payment sufficient? And how do you feel about yourself as you respond in this manner? These words aren't meant to be judgmental or harsh. They are words coming from the deep concern over the pain people have inflicted upon themselves by holding onto and collecting hurts from their interaction with their partner. I would like to see couples live a life free from lingering pain. As Lewis Smedes puts it:

> For two people who are coming together after a falling out, truthfulness requires a promise made and a promise

> meant to be kept. Those who hurt you must return to you with a promise that they will not hurt you again; and you need to believe that they intend to keep the promise they make. They cannot offer you a guarantee; they cannot be depended on the way you might reply on a computer or a well-trained dog. They are ordinary, fallible human beings; they are not God. You lay a bet on them; you need to take a risk.[2]

What do you want? Do you want to hang on to that hurt festering inside you and slowly building a pool of bitterness? Will you hang on to the pain that will consume your joy and belief in Christ's power and presence?

Some of our hurt stems from the uncalled for behavior and words of our partner. Some of it stems from our own perception and predisposition to be hurt. This comes from the unresolved issues in our past. Frequently I will hear a spouse say to his or her partner, "You're just too sensitive!" And that is often true. But telling a person this doesn't bring about a change. There is a reason for sensitivity. And at this point the person is "too" sensitive, but with the help of Jesus Christ he or she can take the steps necessary to change. (For assistance with issues from the past and oversensitivity, please see my book, *Making Peace with Your Past,* Fleming H. Revell, Publisher).

Why did your partner hurt you during your conflicts? There are many reasons. I have heard some partners admit, "I meant to hurt him. He deserved to feel the pain. For what he has done to me, he deserved it! At that point I didn't care." Sometimes this happens, but not as frequently as we tend to believe.

Some partners hurt each other because they have never learned to control what they say or do. Self-control, however, is one of the fruits of the Spirit as mentioned in Galatians 5.

Some hurt the other person because of frustrations that spill over onto their partner. Anger directed toward something else becomes a misguided missile which explodes on their loved one.

How can you assist your partner in overcoming the hurt he or she has experienced in your relationship? Quite simply, apologize and ask forgiveness. You don't have to be totally at fault to do this either. Apologizing and asking forgiveness is focusing upon your own actions and responses without regard for your partner's. In a conflict I need to be more aware of how I have acted wrongly than whatever my spouse has done wrong.

The factor most often omitted in apologizing and asking forgiveness is repentance. This involves renouncing what I did before and committing myself to what I will do in the future.

Therefore the first step in this process is to acknowledge our wrongdoing. I need to acknowledge it first of all to myself, then to God and then to my partner. The second step is to assess its impact. In southern California we have many areas of landfill which are now seeping dangerous industrial waste and pollution. An assessment impact study is frequently undertaken to determine the danger, damage and long-lasting effects. But also involved with this is a proposal for cleanup procedures.

In my counseling office a husband realized what he had done when he and his wife disagreed. Without a word from me he turned to his wife and said, "I guess I'm kind of slow. It's taken me awhile to realize how I've offended you with my sarcasm and put-downs when we disagree. I'm sure this has had an effect upon your feelings about yourself and your love for me. I am apologizing to you for this and asking your forgiveness for the hurt I have caused. I also want you to know that in the future I will not do this to you. In place of this I am going to ask you more questions, consider what you say even if it takes me a few seconds to do this, not assume that you are attacking me. I'm going to listen to you. We may not always agree but it will be less painful."

After he said this, his wife thanked him, stood up, went over to him and kissed him with tears running down her face. Then she returned to her chair and said to him, "I appreciate the insight, growth and commitment I've just seen in you. I would like to assist you by asking the steps you will take to ensure this new commitment."

He thought a minute, grinned and said, "I think I remember some counselor making a few suggestions about how to change." He paused and winked at me and we both grinned. "I'm going to write out my new plan, read it aloud by myself morning and evening for thirty days and if June would be willing to role-play some conversations with me, we could practice this new approach together. I think that would help. And if I ever tend to lapse into my old ways for some reason, I would appreciate it June if you would just hold up one hand and say, 'Where's my new style husband?' That will help call me back to my new program."

This couple made the necessary changes. Notice the steps involved in what this man did.

1. He identified specifically what he had done wrong.
2. He acknowledged the effect of his behavior upon his wife.
3. He asked forgiveness in his apology.
4. He stated what he would be doing in the future that was different.
5. He developed a specific plan to make the changes.
6. He gave his wife permission, if needed, to call him back to his new plan.

Most of us do not intend to hurt our spouses and to repeat behavior which disgusts them. We do need to open the door for them to protect themselves from our old behavior.

Recently I heard of a unique safeguard one husband created to protect his wife from his angry outbursts. Whenever she shared some bad news with him, he would become irate. But he was disgusted with himself and wanted to stop. So he told her that if she is ever fearful that he might become angry over some bad news, she should warn him that it's a bad news item. Then when he asks her to tell him, she should go to the refrigerator, take a raw egg, hold it over his head while she shares the bad news, and then crack it open if he becomes angry. He later referred to this shift of power as the "egg drop soup" approach. And of course you can guess the outcome. They never had to use the egg.[3]

If hurt comes easily to you, perhaps this honest example from the life of a husband will give you some help and direction for a different way to respond.

> I'm supersensitive to having a fault pointed out in me. One day my wife, Ruth, told me that I had dominated a conversation we held with a friend, and that I had not given our friend a chance to speak her mind.

At first impulse I wanted to defend myself, but I deliberately held back and quickly prayed in silence, "Thank You, God, for allowing Ruth to mention this to me. Is there something here You want me to learn?" After a second or two, I realized that I agreed with her. I took a giant step forward for me and deliberately said, "I think you're right."

In my mind I had done all that anyone could reasonably expect of me at that point. I had gone the second, third, and fourth miles with Ruth, and expected her to say, "Okay," and drop the subject. Instead, she continued, "Yes, I think I am right because Martha needed a chance to talk. She was all bottled up with feelings, and you didn't give her a chance to express them."

That statement from Ruth, even though she said it calmly and kindly, caused my pain. I felt humiliated and burned, telling myself that Ruth wanted to roast me for a crime already confessed and forgiven.

Ruth and I had discussed this pattern between us and my effort to change my part in it. Therefore, this time I did not retaliate with anger as I had done in the past, always to Ruth's bewilderment. I realized that she did not intend to singe me after I said that I agreed with her. In fact, her continuing to talk had almost nothing to do with me. She merely wanted to further clarify her own thoughts on the incident by expressing them aloud to me. I relabeled her action from "roasting me" to "thinking out loud." Then I felt better toward her.

By error, I tend to assume that Ruth expects some further response from me. I imagine that she wants me to crawl on my hands and knees, confess that I am wicked and terrible, and vow I'll never do it again. She doesn't want that. She just wants to put her thoughts together. If anything, she wants from me only permission to assemble her thoughts, say them, and find relief. Maybe at most she would like a grunt from me, or perhaps, "I'm with you, honey."[4]

What do you do with hurt that is either fresh from the most recent disagreement or the years of accumulated abuse? Face it, admit it and throw away the shovel that you might be tempted to use to bury the feelings. If your feelings are not allowed to drain, they fester and expand and one day they explode like throwing an aerosol can into a fire!

But what if it's difficult to express those feelings? Imagine yourself on a stage and you are telling the sympathetic audience how you feel about the conflicts and how you feel *after* the conflicts. The audience is filled with empathy and is there just to listen. Tell them how you feel hurt, wronged, angry, rejected and so on. Then take some paper and write out how you feel. Make a diary or a journal or write a letter to your spouse (which you do not mail) sharing both your feelings and what you would like to be different in your relationship. Be sure not to hold back your feelings since you're not going to mail the letter.

By facing your feelings you can come to the next step. This is analyzing the feeling and discovering the thoughts that helped to create it. Letting loose of the hurts stemming from conflicts means you are requesting a good case of amnesia. That's right—learning to forget. We don't really forget anything we ever experience, but perhaps Webster's definition of *forget* can give us some insight and help. Forget means "to lose the remembrance of . . . to treat with inattention or disregard . . . overlook . . . to cease remembering or noticing . . . to fail to become mindful at the proper time."

There it is! Action on our part to let the offense drop out of our lives. At first there is emotional remembering in which you feel the hurt each time you remember. But in time it becomes historical remembering in which you know it happened, but it no longer impacts your life. That's forgetting the hurts you didn't deserve. Our Savior received hurts He didn't deserve either. He chose to take upon Himself the burdens and hurts of mankind. Through what He did we have new life. Through your hurts there can be the opportunity for growth.

Hurt is often like the aftermath of a fire. We feel destroyed just as a fire destroys the beautiful forest. Remember the story at the beginning of this chapter concerning our hiking to Bradley Lake? The foliage within that forest was breathtaking. But in August of 1985 lightning struck and a fire raged through trees and brush. The next time I saw the area I was taken aback and dejected by the ugly black skeletons of trees. Where there was once life and beauty only waste remained.

A year later, however, as I walked the trail I was just as surprised to see pushing up through the ashes new growth, healthy and alive. Wildflowers such as paintbrush and columbine poked their way through the blackened soil. Each year the area is looking less and less like a site of destruction as the new life begins to take over and eradicate the scars. As new vegetation arises from the ground, you can overcome the hurt and see yourself and your spouse in a new light—a light made possible because of the presence of Jesus Christ alive and real in your lives.

Life-Changers

Remember to forget your hurts.

Don't allow your life to be dominated by collected hurts.

Identify what you have *done, its effect upon your partner, ask forgiveness, share what you will do in the future and develop a plan to change.*

Notes

Chapter 1

1. Francine Klagsbrun, *Married People Staying Together in the Age of Divorce* (New York: Bantam Books, 1985) 279–295 adapted.
2. Word Biblical Commentary, *Philippians*, Gerald F. Hawthorne (Waco, TX: Word Books, 1983), adapted.
3. Lewis Smedes, *How Can It Be All Right When Everything Is All Wrong?* (San Francisco; Harper & Row, 1982) 11.
4. Maxine Rock, *The Marriage Map* (Atlanta: Peachtree Publishers, 1986) 78–79.
5. Mike Mason, *The Mystery of Marriage* (Portland, OR: Multnomah Press, 1985) 55–56.
6. Mel Krantzler, *Creative Marriage* (New York: McGraw Hill Book Co., 1981) 9.

Chapter 2

1. Ernie Larsen, *Stage II Recovery* (San Francisco: Harper and Row, 1987), 34–37 adapted.
2. Larsen, 38–45 adapted.
3. Dr. Kevin Leman, *The Pleasers—Women Who Can't Say No—And The Men Who Control Them* (Old Tappan, NJ: Fleming H. Revell, 1987) 21–23, adapted.
4. Leman, 37.
5. David Viscott, *I Love You, Let's Work It Out* (New York: Simon & Schuster, 1987) 125–126 adapted.
6. Viscott, p 133–144 adapted.
7. Leman, 188–189.

Chapter 3

1. Francine Klagsbrun, *Married People: Staying Together in the Age of Divorce* (New York: Bantam Books, 1985) 84–85 adapted.
2. Martin H. Padovani, *Healing Wounded Emotions* (Mystic, CT: Twenty-Third Publications, 1987), 88–89.
3. Charles Swindoll, *Living above the Level of Mediocrity* (Waco, TX: Word Books, 1987), 19.

4. Lloyd John Ogilive, *God's Will in My Life* (Eugene, Oregon: Harvest House, 1982), 136.
5. Ogilvie, 144–145.
6. Swindoll, 26.
7. Swindoll, 29.

Chapter 4

1. Daniel Goleman, *Two Views of Marriage Explored: His and Hers* (The New York Times, 1 April 1986), C1 adapted.
2. Philip Blumstein, Ph.D. and Pepper Schwartz, Ph.D., *American Couples* (New York: Pocket Books, 1985), adapted and no page number given from source.
3. Miriam Arond and Samuel L. Pauker, *The First Year of Marriage* (New York: Warner Books, 1987), 164, 165 adapted.
4. Michael E. McGill, Ph.D. *Changing Him, Changing Her* (New York: Simon & Schuster, 1982) 96–128 adapted.

Chapter 5

1. Miriam Arond and Samuel L. Pauker, *The First Year of Marriage* (New York: Warner Books, 1987) 188, 189 adapted.
2. Philip Yancey, *After the Wedding* (Waco, TX: Word Books, 1976) 29, 30.
3. Arond and Pauker, 84, 89 adapted.
4. David Viscott, *I Love You, Let's Work It Out* (New York: Simon and Schuster, 1987) 89 adapted.
5. Viscott, 85 (adapted from this work and this author's procedures).
6. Viscott, 176–177.

Chapter 6

1. Hoopes, M. & Harper, J. *Birth Order Roles and Sibling Patterns in Individual and Family Therapy* (Rockville, Maryland: Aspen Publishers, 1987), 35–57; 84–89; 107–122 adapted.

Chapter 7

1. Joyce Brothers, *What Every Woman Should Know about Men* (New York: Ballantine Books, 1981) 31–34 adapted. Jacquelyn Wonder and Priscilla Donovan, *Whole Brain Thinking* (New York: William Morrow and Company, 1984) 18–34 adapted.

Chapter 8

1. Susan M. Campbell, *Beyond the Power Struggle* (San Luis Obispo, CA: Impact Publishers, 1984) 50–55: 70–72.
2. Ruth McRoberts Ward, *Self-Esteem: Gift from God* (Grand Rapids: Baker Book House, 1984) 42–69 & 147–193 adapted.

Chapter 9

1. William J. Lederer, *Marital Choices* (New York: W.W. Norton & Co., 1987) 164–166 adapted.

2. Francine Klagsburn, *Married People: Staying Together in the Age of Divorce* (New York: Bantam Books, 1985) 50–68 adapted.

3. Miriam Arond & Samuel Pauker, *The First Year of Marriage* (New York: Warner Books, 1987), 104–106 adapted.

4. Arond & Parker, 106–107.

5. Arond & Parker, 108–109 adapted.

6. Dr. Carlfred Broderick, *Couples—How to Confront Problems and Maintain Loving Relationships* (New York: Simon & Schuster, 1979) 101–106 adapted.

7. Robert A. Schuller, *Power to Grow Beyond Yourself* (Old Tappan, NJ: Fleming H. Revell, 1987) 175–176.

8. Broderick, 118–125 adapted.

Chapter 10

1. Baucom, D. & Beckham, E. & Lester, G., "Implementation of Behavioral Marital Therapy," *Journal of Marital & Family Therapy, American Association for Marriage & Family Therapy* (Upland Co. Vol. 6 # 2, April 1980), 191–194.

2. Viscott, David, *I Love You, Let's Work It Out* (New York: Simon and Schuster, 1987) 81 adapted.

Chapter 11

1. Richard P. Walters, *Anger: Yours and Mine and What to Do About It* (Grand Rapids: Zondervan Publishing House, 1981) 139.

2. Carol Travis, *Anger—The Misunderstood Emotion* (New York: Simon and Schuster, 1982), 220–221 adapted.

3. David Mace, *Marital Intimacy and the Deadly Love-Anger Cycle,* Journal of Marriage and Family Counseling, April 1976, 136.

Chapter 12

1. J. Allan Petersen, *The Myth of the Greener Grass* (Wheaton: Tyndale House Publishers, 1985) 81 adapted.

2. Petersen, 85.

3. Dr. James Dobson, "The Lure of Infidelity," a Focus On The Family tape.

4. Peter Kreitler with Bill Burns, *Affair Prevention* (New York: MacMillan Publishing Co. 1981) 68.

5. Ella Wheeler Wilcox, "An Unfaithful Wife to Her Husband," *Whatever Is Best,* Collection of Poems (Boulder, CO: Blue Mountain Arts, Inc, 1975) 62 & 63.

6. Mike Mason, *The Mystery of Marriage* (Portland, OR: Multnomah Press, 1985), 94.

7. Mason, 95.
8. Mason, 97–98.

Chapter 13

1. Charles R. Swindoll, *Living above the Level of Mediocrity* (Waco, TX: Word Books, 1987), 100.

Chapter 14

1. Lewis B. Smedes, *Forgive and Forget* (San Francisco: Harper and Row, 1984) xi.
2. Smedes, 34.
3. Dennis L. Gibson, *The Strong-Willed Adult* (Grand Rapids: Baker Book House, 1987) 107–112, adapted.
4. Gibson, 77–78.

Study Guide

How to Use This Book

The questions and exercises in this study guide are designed for individual study which will in turn lead to group interaction. Thus, they may be used either as a guide for individual meditation or group discussion. During your first group meeting we suggest that you set aside a few minutes at the outset in which individual group members introduce themselves.

You may want to begin each meeting with a different question designed to cause participants to think and share information not previously considered. Use just one question, but go around your group and ask each person to share. Here are some suggested questions:

1. What is your favorite smell?
2. What is your favorite sight?
3. What is your favorite touch?
4. What is your favorite taste?
5. What is your favorite sound?
6. What do your favorite senses say about you?
7. What is the first gift that you can remember receiving?
8. What are two adjectives you would use to describe yourself?
9. What two adjectives would your spouse use to describe you?
10. In the past six months, what passage of scripture has meant the most to you and why?
11. If you could reach out and heal someone one day, who would it be?

If possible, it is a good idea to rotate leadership responsibility among the group members. However, if one individual is particularly gifted as a discussion leader, elect or appoint that person to guide the discussions each week. Remember, the leader's responsibility is simply to guide the discussion and stimulate interaction. He or she should never dominate the proceedings. Rather, the leader should encourage all members of the group to participate, expressing their individual views. He or she should seek to keep the discussion on track, but encourage lively discussion.

If one of the purposes of your group meeting is to create a

caring community, it is a good idea to set aside some time for sharing individual concerns and prayers for one another. This can take the form of both silent and spoken petitions and praise.

Chapter 1. There Is Relief in Sight

1. Using the author's "weather report" analogy, how would you characterize your marriage?
2. Review the seven characteristics of a "healthy marriage." Which of the seven are already being worked out in your marriage? Which do you feel you need to work on?
3. Do you agree with the author's "judgment of joy" in terms of your marriage relationship? Can you "consider" trials a joyous experience?
4. Re-read Mike Mason's "prescription" for a happy, fulfilling marriage in this chapter. Has this happened in your marriage?
5. Mel Krantzler says: "Every couple has the personal power to re-create their marriage and transform it into the kind of loving relationship that they want with each other." What does he mean by this? Do you agree with him?

Chapter 2. Who's Running Your Life?

1. Do you feel that your habits master you?
2. Wright says: "You cannot expect different results from the same old behavior—new results come from new behavior!" Think about the truth of this statement and discuss its ramifications for you.
3. What are the six common characteristics of "pleasers"? Do you agree that women more often than men are pleasers?
4. What are the five kinds of "pleasers" that Leman has discovered?
5. Contrast the characteristics of pleasers and controllers. Is it possible to be both?

Chapter 3. "There Has to Be a Better Way!"

1. What are some of the common reasons that people resist change in their lives?
2. Do you agree that change is inevitable?
3. What would you like to change in your marital relationship?
4. What would you like your spouse to change?
5. Where must change begin?
6. What effect does praising God have in a marriage?
7. What effect does memorizing Scripture have on a marriage?

Chapter 4. There's a Reason for Your Conflicts

1. "In a conflict," says Wright, "the difficulty is not the issue but the people involved." What does he mean?
2. What are the three concerns women have about communication?

3. What other concerns most frequently surface?
4. Do you agree that sexual expectations differ between the sexes?
5. Why does the lack of intimacy in marriage generate conflict?
6. How do differing attitudes toward money impact the marriage relationship?
7. Ask yourself the questions on the last page of this chapter. How do you feel about your answers?

Chapter 5. Yes, There Are Solutions!

1. The author says, "Conflict is nothing more than a mismanaged problem." Do you agree?
2. What are the four principles of handling marital problems listed by the author?
3. The author talks about "lookers" and "leapers." Which are you? Which is your spouse? How does this help you in looking at your marriage?
4. How does your work,.and your attitude toward it, affect your marriage?
5. Look back at and analyze your answers to the quiz in this chapter. Can you talk to your spouse about it?
6. Have you ever tried to keep a Conflict Growth Notebook? Could you share with your spouse as is suggested?

Chapter 6. You Are Different . . . and There Are Good Reasons!

1. Do you consider your spouse your best friend?
2. Do you know why you are the way you are?
3. Do you know why your spouse is the way he/she is?
4. "John's sense of self-esteem is built on achievements and how he appears in the eyes of others around him." Are men usually this way? How about women?
5. What did you write in blanks 9 and 10 of the exercise in this chapter?
6. How does knowing the birth order of a person help in understanding him or her?
7. Review the assignment on the last page of this chapter. How did it help you in your marriage relationship?

Chapter 7. Differences: Are You a Thinker or a Feeler?

1. Are men usually "thinkers" and women "feelers"?
2. Re-read the author's description of the brain, particularly the differences between the male and the female. Does this help you understand why men are the way they are—and women too?
3. Do you agree that women enjoy certain advantages in the way they use their brains?
4. Do you agree that women are usually more perceptive about people than are men?
5. How do you and your spouse balance on the scale at the end of this chapter?

Chapter 8. How Would You Like to Be Married to Someone Just Like You?

1. Where do you place yourself on the Saver-Spender scale? Your spouse?
2. Where do you place yourself on the Inner-Outer scale? Your spouse?
3. Where do you place yourself on the Organized-Spontaneous scale? Your spouse?
4. As you review the graphs in this chapter, does it help you better understand your spouse? Yourself?
5. Would you like to be married to someone exactly like you?

Chapter 9. Give Me Power

1. "The more you struggle for power, the less you have!" Do you agree with this premise? How does it apply particularly to the marital relationship?
2. "Power struggles can easily emerge when both husband and wife have their own careers." How do power struggles play themselves out in your relationship?
3. "Which marriages survive when the woman earns more or achieves more than her husband?" How did you (or would you) answer this question?
4. Re-read Joe and Sadi's story. Are their rather capricious arguments typical of most marriages? Your marriage?
5. Find yourself in one of the "power styles" described in this chapter. Identify your spouse's position.
6. Identify the "vicious circles" operating in your marriage.

Chapter 10. It's Not What You Say . . . or Is It?

1. How did you feel about Kurt and Heather's conversation at the beginning of the chapter? With whom could you best identify?
2. Wright says that "Kurt and Heather communicate as though life is a contest." How would you describe the way you and your spouse communicate?
3. "Many marriages are battlefields littered with the remains of men and women who never came to the peace table to negotiate a settlement." Do you agree with this assessment?
4. Review the other six "rules" and apply them to your situation.
5. Read the continuation of Kurt and Heather's conversation. How does it differ from the conversation at the beginning of the chapter?
6. Read and apply the principles in the marriage covenant at the end of the chapter. Do these work for you?

Chapter 11 Anger—a Conflict Crippler!

1. This is a strange chapter title. Why would anger "cripple" conflict?
2. What are the "two R's" of conflict?
3. How do you and your spouse handle anger? When you underreact, what do you do? When you overreact, what do you do?
3. How do you react to these "truths about anger": "Anger is not the prob-

lem or the main emotion. Anger is a symptom!" "Expressing your anger to your partner does not lessen your anger. It usually increases it!" "How you use your anger was learned. This means you can learn a new response and get it under control." "Your partner is not responsible for making you angry. You are!"
4. How does frustration figure in the anger quotient?
5. Wright says, "Remember, it isn't your partner who *makes* you angry. It's your inner response . . . that creates the anger." Discuss.
6. Review Janice and John's situation. With whom do you identify?
7. Re-read and use the three points under the "delaying process." Do they help you?
8. What are David Mace's two positive ways to control anger?
9. "More marriages today are dying from silence than from violence." Think about and discuss.

Chapter 12. The Breaking of a Vow

1. Do you agree with Wright's description of an affair?
2. Have you been guilty of such an action?
3. Review the reasons why an affair occurs. Are any of these present in your relationship?
4. "Unresolved conflicts are the breeding ground for the mind to cooperate with the temptations of life." Discuss.
5. Read Dr. James Dobson's comment in this chapter and discuss.
6. "Affairs are a reaction to a marital vacuum." Do you agree?
7. Re-read Mike Mason's thoughts on the marriage vows. Does this approach "work" for you?

Chapter 13. "I Believe in You"

1. To "encourage," says Wright, means to "expect the best from your spouse." Have you tried this approach?
2. How did you do in the personal "encouraging" quiz in this chapter? Did you have trouble coming up with six answers to each question or statement?
3. How about the quiz on your partner's strengths or capabilities?
4. Could you formulate a plan based on these exercises?
5. "Encouragement means not taking your partner for granted." Is this too simplistic?
6. Read Susan and Hank's story. What was Hank really doing for Susan?
7. Read Sheri and Tony's story. Why does Tony react to her as he does?
8. "How can you relabel this to give your spouse the benefit of a doubt?" Apply this principle to one aspect of your marriage. What happened when you did?

Chapter 14. Let Loose of Your Hurt

1. Are you a collector? What do you collect?
2. Read Dr. Lewis Smedes' description of the way people react. Where do you find yourself?

3. "If I forgive . . . I make myself vulnerable and open to being hurt again." Discuss.
4. Review the six steps the husband in this chapter took to mend the rift in his marriage. If you were the wife in this situation, how would you react?
5. Read the author's concluding "forest fire" illustration. Has your marriage ever had to weather such an experience? If so, what did you do with your hurts—forgive or forget?

H. NORMAN WRIGHT is a widely known marriage counselor, trainer of counselors, and longtime professor of counseling at Biola University and Talbot Seminary. He is founder and director of Christian Marriage Enrichment and Family Counseling and Enrichment in Santa Ana, California. His more than fifty books include *Communication: Key to Your Marriage, Crisis Counseling, How to Have a Creative Crisis,* and *Understanding the Man in Your Life.* He is also the author of *Self-Talk, Imagery and Prayer* in the Resources for Christian Counseling series.